MW00415244

Stinging Nettle

As told by Vladimir and Margaretha Fortenbacher

Interviewed by Johanna Fortenbacher

PUBLISHED BY WESTVIEW, INC.
KINGSTON SPRINGS, TENNESSEE

Ideas into Books®
W E S T V I E W
P.O. Box 605
Kingston Springs, TN 37082
www.publishedbywestview.com

ISBN 978-1-62880-012-8

First edition, January 2014

Printed in the United States of America on acid free paper.

Preface

At the completion of *Stinging Nettle,* Vladimir and Margaretha Fortenbacher passed their eighty-second birthdays. They are amazed at God's faithfulness and where He has taken them along life's journey. Vladimir and Margaretha each had their own personal experiences of living in Eastern Europe during WWII before they voyaged across the Atlantic Ocean to Canada, the land of opportunity.

In their search for greener grass, they found a silver lining. The silver lining didn't come in the form of money or material possessions, but in the discovery that each day was a gift from God to treasure and that nothing should be taken for granted.

This book is written as a commemorative for Vladimir and Margaretha to pass on to their 12 children, their grandchildren, and future Fortenbacher generations to help them understand their roots and heritage of faith. We, their children, had only heard bits and pieces of their stories while growing up, and we had no idea of the degree to which our parents had suffered through WWII.

Some of their experiences are difficult for us to comprehend because we live in the freedom of another time and place. As Vladimir and Margaretha recalled these events in their lives from more than 70 years ago, they didn't have a full understanding of the political background. For them, it was "just the way it happened."

As you read their chronicles, it is our hope that you, too, will find the silver lining beyond your own difficult circumstances, and will be inspired to leave a legacy in the lives you touch.

All proceeds from *Stinging Nettle* will be used towards Christian-based world relief projects. This book is dedicated to individuals and organizations that relieve suffering caused by displacement from natural disasters, war, and unjust imprisonment.

"And whosoever shall give to drink unto one of these little ones a cup of cold water only in the name of a disciple, verily I say unto you, he shall in no wise lose his reward."

(Matthew 10:42) KJV

Acknowledgments

Kendra Ramsier was the one who "got the ball rolling" on *Stinging Nettle*. She is a former teacher and family friend from Rittman, OH who has experience in writing and publishing. Kendra was motivated by Vladimir's and Margaretha's history and felt that their stories would help people understand what life is like outside the "safe bubble of America." Johanna Fortenbacher interviewed Vladimir and Margaretha while Kendra transcribed her notes over a span of about five years.

The book was at a standstill in 2009 while Kendra was expecting her sixth child and unable to devote any more time to writing. At that point in time, Carola (Fortenbacher) Schlatter had taken a break from her nursing studies. Vladimir and Margaretha had expressed how they wished that the book could somehow get done because many relatives and friends had heard about their "story in the making" and were anxious to read of their accounts. Feeling God's direction to take the book to completion, Carola spent countless hours making additions and revisions to *Stinging Nettle*. As the daughter of Vladimir and Margaretha, she was able to bring in a personal perspective.

Carola and Kendra would like to thank their family members and friends who have supported their endeavors. They would also like to acknowledge individuals who have made contributions to *Stinging Nettle*. Johanna Fortenbacher was the primary interviewer and she also helped with details such as proofreading and investigating the spelling of names and places. Rosanne (Fortenbacher) Graf photographed the book cover, designed the cover pages and genealogies, and helped proofread. She also assisted Beth Rufener with the maps of Vladimir's and Margaretha's journeys from their birthplaces to their arrival in Canada.

Ingrid Fortenbacher, Brooklyn Lehner, Marilyn Schubert, Astrid (Fortenbacher) Schlauch, and Barbara (Fortenbacher) Zollinger read through book drafts and gave helpful suggestions. Lydia (Fortenbacher) Graf found the stinging nettle plant and assisted Rosanne with the photography of the cover page. Kathy Bowman photographed the back cover photo of Vladimir and Margaretha, as well as the recent family photo at the end of the book.

PART I
Vladimir's Story

Table of Contents

Furtenbaher Genealogy

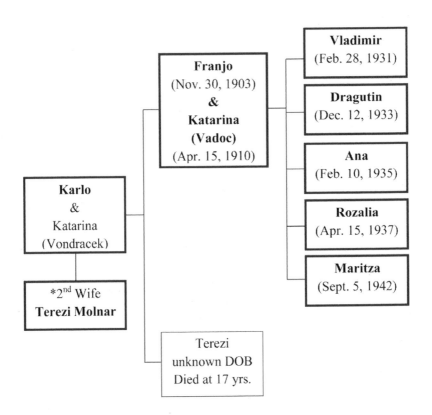

Vladimir
(Feb. 28, 1931)

Dragutin
(Dec. 12, 1933)

Ana
(Feb. 10, 1935)

Rozalia
(Apr. 15, 1937)

Maritza
(Sept. 5, 1942)

Franjo
(Nov. 30, 1903)
&
Katarina
(Vadoc)
(Apr. 15, 1910)

Karlo
&
Katarina
(Vondracek)

*2nd Wife
Terezi Molnar

Terezi
unknown DOB
Died at 17 yrs.

Vadoc Genealogy

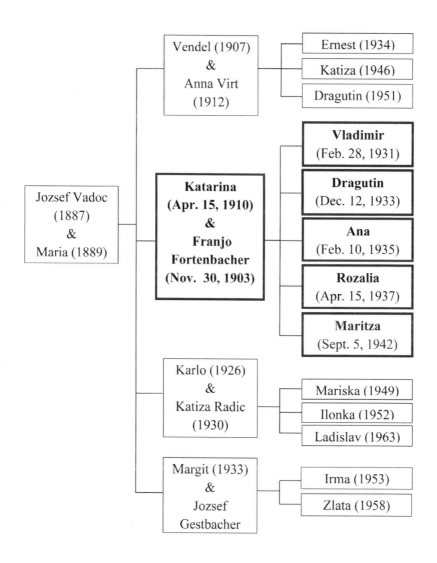

- Jozsef Vadoc (1887) & Maria (1889)
  - Vendel (1907) & Anna Virt (1912)
    - Ernest (1934)
    - Katiza (1946)
    - Dragutin (1951)
  - **Katarina (Apr. 15, 1910) & Franjo Fortenbacher (Nov. 30, 1903)**
    - **Vladimir (Feb. 28, 1931)**
    - **Dragutin (Dec. 12, 1933)**
    - **Ana (Feb. 10, 1935)**
    - **Rozalia (Apr. 15, 1937)**
    - **Maritza (Sept. 5, 1942)**
  - Karlo (1926) & Katiza Radic (1930)
    - Mariska (1949)
    - Ilonka (1952)
    - Ladislav (1963)
  - Margit (1933) & Jozsef Gestbacher
    - Irma (1953)
    - Zlata (1958)

Introduction to Vladimir's Story

The setting of Vladimir Fortnbaher's story takes place in Golenić, Yugoslavia (present-day Croatia). It begins with his earliest childhood memory at six years old, and provides just a glimpse of his love for horses. Until he turns thirteen, his life is rather uneventful, other than the ethnic tensions that precede WWII. Vladimir's story is fairly easy to follow because it primarily involves his individual family and Fortnbaher grandparents.

Vladimir's great-grandfather had emigrated from Germany to Hungary. Although there aren't any clear family records, the original last name is believed to have been Von Furtenbacher. Vladimir remembered that his father had received a letter in Golenić from relatives in Germany with that same last name.

While living in Hungary, Vladimir's Grandfather Karlo changed the last name to Furtenbaher. When the family later moved to Golenić, Yugoslavia, Grandfather Karlo changed the last name to Fortnbaher. That is how Vladimir recalls spelling his last name in school. Lastly, Vladimir's father changed the last name to Fortenbacher while the family was living as refugees during WWII. All of these spelling changes were made so the family would fit in better with the local people.

Vladimir refers to his father as "Tata" and his mother as "Mama." Asterisks within the chapters are an indication of a change in topic or time frame. There are also editor notes at the end of some of the chapters to give background or to explain situations within the story.

SECTION ONE:

Vladimir's Early Years

1

Golenić
1937

Six-year-old Vladimir carried the heavy feed bucket as he and his brother Dragutin made their way through the barn towards the horse stalls. Behind them, a few chickens pecked hungrily at the kernels of grain that had spilled from the bucket. It wouldn't be long before Dragutin would also be given responsibilities around the farm. Dragutin was a couple of years younger than Vladimir, and he often tagged along during chore times.

After setting the feed bucket down in one of the stalls, Vladimir shooed the chickens away with his hand. Feeding the horses was his favorite chore—he never tired of admiring the majestic creatures, and he sought every opportunity to be around them. As Vladimir began scooping out grain from the feed bucket, his keen eyes saw movement in the distance. It was a rider on a horse. Perhaps someone was coming to look at the gray colt. He ran swiftly to tell Tata.

Vladimir recognized the gentleman on horseback as he eventually made his way into their farmyard. And it was true— he had indeed come to look at the gray colt. Tata was well-known in the region for his horse breeding, and the gray colt would be the third foal sold since early spring. Vladimir was relieved that he had just cleaned out the horse stalls!

Tata placed a leather halter over the gray colt's ears before securing it firmly on the side of his face and leading the colt out into the farmyard. Vladimir listened as his father and the gentleman discussed prices and the colt's pedigree. The gentleman ran his hand down the colt's mane, checked its teeth, and measured the flanks. Vladimir smiled to himself as he noticed the slight nod of the gentleman's head as he talked with Tata. Most likely it meant that they had made another sale.

"Franjo, what do you suppose is going to happen when ..."

What on earth was the gentleman talking about? Vladimir motioned impatiently to Dragutin to stop teasing the rooster. They were causing too much racket, and he just couldn't quite grasp the content of the adults' conversation.

After the gentleman left the farmyard, Vladimir retraced his steps to the horse stall. He hurried to finish his chores before dark. Besides completing the horse chores, Vladimir still needed to gather the eggs and find a handful of stinging nettle plants.

Springtime was the growing season for stinging nettle. After the perennial plants were gathered, they were ground up with the cornmeal to feed the flock of noisy ducks and geese. Tata and Mama had taught him that stinging nettle was the secret to making the meat tender. Before cutting off the plants with a knife, the stems had to be held just right to prevent getting stung by the spiny needles. If Vladimir rushed too quickly, he paid dearly with sore fingers.

Mama already had the oil lamps lit by the time he reached the house. It seemed to Vladimir that Mama never sat down. She was constantly moving about, whether she was sweeping the floors, preparing the meals, gardening, or going about her endless chores around the house and farm.

Tata had been the mayor of Golenić for as long as Vladimir could remember. Located near the Hungarian border, Golenić was a village in the Croatian province of Yugoslavia. Tata attended meetings at the city hall and took care of the village's paperwork. It wasn't uncommon to see villagers stop by at their farm to discuss important matters with Tata.

Vladimir, born on February 28, 1931, was the oldest of the Fortnbaher children. He was followed by four-year-old Dragutin, two-year-old Ana, and baby Rozalia. Their three-room home didn't have much space for running or chasing. If the boys became too rowdy, a sharp word or swift swat on their backsides from Tata's hand quickly brought everything under control. Tata believed that strict discipline led to productive adults.

But even though the Fortnbaher home was modest, it held everything that their family needed. Grandfather Karlo Fortnbaher and Stepgrandmother Terezi also lived with Vladimir's family on their small farm nestled among the hills and trees in Golenić. As the family worked together, they conversed in Hungarian. It appeared that their simple life would always continue that way.

The only threat to their peace was the constant tension between ethnic groups. The Serbians in the surrounding communities were not friendly with the Croatians and the Hungarians from the village of Golenić. But in their rural and remote geographic region, the Golenić villagers had little knowledge of the political turmoil brewing around them.

* * * * * * * * * * * * * * * * * *

EDITOR NOTE: Franjo Fortnbaher was born in Sladojevci, Croatia. He was raised in the Catholic faith, and he was fluent in both the Croatian and Hungarian languages. Grandfather Karlo had a German background and his deceased wife was of Czechoslovakian descent. Stepgrandmother Terezi was Hungarian.

Katarina Vadoc was born in the village of Budakovac, Croatia. Her ethnicity was primarily Hungarian, and she was also raised in the Catholic faith. The village of Budakovac was located about 30 kilometers from Golenić. Katarina primarily kept in touch with her family through letters because visits there occurred only about once a year.

* * * * * * * * * * * * * * * * * *

13

EDITOR NOTE: The village of Golenić had approximately 30–32 houses during Vladimir's early childhood. Most of the villagers were from Hungarian and Croatian backgrounds, but several German and Serbian families also lived there. Around the start of WWII, about 20 Croatian families from a nearby district moved into Golenić. Those Croatian families worked for a baron who owned a lot of land.

At the time of this writing, Golenić, Croatia could be viewed on Google Maps. It is interesting to note that the road ends in Golenić. The village was in the middle of nowhere, and it appears that the houses have all been torn down.

Wedding photo of Franjo Fortnbaher and Katarina
Vadoc, March 1930

2

Trouble
1938

Vladimir was picking plums and dropping them into his pail with a steady rhythm. Beside him, Tata was filling his pail up even more quickly. Plum trees were just one of the varieties of fruit trees that grew in the Fortnbaher orchard, and Grandfather Karlo was hoping to make some fine whiskey with this year's plum harvest.

Both Vladimir and Tata turned their heads at the sound of horses' hooves. Two men on horseback had come to an abrupt halt just beyond the thicket of plum trees. Vladimir instantly recognized the police hats and uniforms. Tata stepped off of the ladder and set his nearly filled pail under the plum tree. Vladimir also stepped off of the ladder, hesitantly holding onto his pail of plums as he followed Tata to the edge of the orchard. Tata continued walking until he was within close range of the policemen, who remained on their majestic-looking horses. Why were they here? Was something wrong?

"Sir," one of the policemen addressed Tata. "We're here to discuss the accident that happened last week."

How well Vladimir remembered Tata describing the accident! Tata had been asked to chauffeur a baron, a royal overseer of land in the nearby region. Vladimir had few associations with rich and royal men, and so each meeting made a significant impression on him.

Vladimir recalled the pair of dark brown, pristine horses that had belonged to the baron. Their bridles glistened in the sunlight with every shake of their manes. The baron had been sitting beside Tata on the cushioned wagon seat. How proud

16

Vladimir remembered feeling as he watched Tata expertly handling the horses!

Unfortunately, all pomp and grandeur had gone awry when the horses turned too sharply. Tata said that it had all happened so fast. First one of the horse's legs had slipped from underneath him. Then both of the horses collapsed and became entangled within the reins. Tata had worked as fast as he could to untangle the reins and calm the horses, but it soon became apparent that the only solution was to cut the bridles. Eventually the animals were back on their feet. From that point on, Tata had tried his best to complete the tour with the baron.

The incident was not the end of Tata's troubles. Later it was discovered that some of the expensive pelts from the back of the wagon were missing. When the horses had struggled to regain their footing, they caused the wagon to overturn, and some people stopped to help. Apparently, while Tata was focused on the horses, someone must have stolen some of the pelts from the wagon. Tata was very concerned that he could be blamed.

As the police questioned Tata, Vladimir tried hard to make out what they were saying. " . . . those pelts?" one of the policemen asked.

Tata shook his head solemnly.

"Then where are they?" the policemen demanded.

It was obvious that Tata didn't know, but the policemen didn't let up with their questioning.

One of the policemen turned his attention to Vladimir, walking over to where he stood at the edge of the orchard. The policeman crouched down to Vladimir's height. His dark eyes seemed to soften ever so slightly as he spoke.

"Son, do you remember when your father was driving the baron's horses and they became entangled?"

Even though Vladimir was trembling on the inside, he nodded.

"The back of the wagon was filled with expensive pelts. Some of those pelts are now missing. Have you seen them?"

Vladimir solemnly shook his head and replied, "No."

The policeman's eyes became more intense. "Did your father take them?"

Mama had advised Vladimir to always tell the truth. Now, as the policeman's eyes seemed to bore right through him, Vladimir again shook his head.

"Listen, young man," the policeman continued, ". . . we need to know." He reached into one of the deep pockets on his jacket and drew out several large coins. "See these? If you can tell us something about the pelts, then you can have all of these coins. Did your father take them?"

Even a boy as young as Vladimir knew that the handful of coins was very valuable. It was more money than he had ever seen! What should he say? Vladimir undoubtedly knew what he needed to do. "No," he firmly stated. "My Tata did not take any of those pelts."

3

School Days
1938

"See the sun? The sun is up. The sun gives us light . . ." Vladimir stared at the line of Croatian words and repeated them over and over in his mind. They were so different from the Hungarian words he had spoken at home for seven years before attending school. The school building was located in the village of Lukovac, a three-and-a-half kilometer walk.

"Grade two," Mr. Kosanovic announced.

Vladimir's shoulders tensed as the 2nd graders filed past the hot wooden stove and lined up by the teacher's desk. The 1st graders would be called out next, and Vladimir still couldn't remember the lines. How he detested this memory work!

Mr. Kosanovic expected order and diligence from his forty-five students. From the youngest 1st grader, to the oldest 5th grader, there was no doubt in their minds that extra noise would not be tolerated, and that their lessons must be completed neatly and quickly. Mr. Kosanovic also tried to keep a firm handle on any ethnic tensions between the Hungarian and Croatian students of Golenić, and the Serbian students from Lukovac.

"Lunchtime!" was a welcomed announcement for Vladimir. His sandwich consisted of homemade bread that was spread with a thick layer of lard, topped with red peppers and smoked meat. It tasted even better after heating it inside the wood stove. Even though it was a very cold December day, he and some other boys looked forward to a quick game of soccer. They ate their lunches as fast as they could before heading outside for recess.

The afternoon school lessons typically began with arithmetic, which Vladimir preferred over reading and memory work. Today, however, they got a break from their daily routine because they had to practice for the school Christmas program. The children who were Serbian Orthodox celebrated Christmas on January 7. Hungarian and Croatian Catholics celebrated Christmas on December 24 and 25.

When school was dismissed, Vladimir gathered up his leather book bag and lunch box before putting on his overcoat. He decided to take the shortcut through the woods because he was anxious to get home. Tonight the family would be decorating their Christmas tree.

Soon Vladimir was beyond the swirling snow of the Lukovac countryside, and the familiar row of houses in the village of Golenić came into view. Vladimir walked past the houses before breaking into a sprint for the final stretch towards the farm. He arrived home breathless and rosy-cheeked.

* * * * * * * * * * * * * * * * * *

EDITOR NOTE: After several of the Fortnbaher children attended school, it became more common for the family to speak Croatian to each other at home. To this day, Vladimir still finds himself figuring math equations in his mind in Croatian as he had been taught in grade school, despite his Hungarian tongue and other languages learned.

4

Outings
1939 – Winter 1940

The Fortnbaher family farm was as self-sufficient as it could be. Staples such as yeast, sugar, or matches were purchased from a little store in the neighboring village of Lukovac. If larger supplies such as a plow were needed, it required an all-day trip to Podravaska Slatina. This city was located approximately 15 kilometers from Golenić.

Vladimir could think of nothing more exciting than to ride along with Tata on a trip to Podravaska Slatina. Compared to the little farming village of Golenić, Podravaska Slatina had real stores with wide streets, and there were always lots of people walking about. Unfortunately, going beyond Lukovac only happened about once or twice a year.

* * * * * * * * * * * * * * * * * * *

On Sunday morning, Vladimir hurried to finish his chores. His family would most likely be visiting another family in the area. The Fortnbaher family usually attended mass only on Easter and Christmas. The church was a 45-minute journey by wagon.

Vladimir kicked the ground with the toe of his boot to determine whether the ground was still frozen. The spring sun had already melted the ice in the creek, so there wouldn't be any skating today. It was just as well—the wires that Vladimir attached to his boots to convert them into ice skates were getting too worn anyways.

Perhaps he and the other children could play soccer today. If the ground was soft enough, they could press sticks into the ground for goal posts, or they could play a game of baseball by using a larger piece of wood for a bat.

Soon Vladimir and his family were seated in the wagon behind their team of horses, Lisa and Sova. Vladimir and Dragutin had gathered some sticks of various sizes for their games. Ana and Rozalia brought along some stones for hopscotch and some balls for juggling.

Several other families also gathered with them at the neighboring farm. All of the children occupied themselves by playing games. Tata and the other men drank whiskey while discussing politics, WWI experiences, and farming developments.

In the evening, someone played an accordion. Young men and women paired up to dance while the younger school children like Vladimir sat on the sidelines and watched. Traditional snacks of popcorn and pumpkin seeds were served by the women. Sundays were carefree days for the Fortnbaher family.

* * * * * * * * * * * * * * * * * *

Every day—especially during harvest time—was filled to capacity by the necessary tasks for daily living. One fall morning Mama had been busy picking, sorting, and packing some fruit and vegetables into a large basket. All of the produce was grown on their land, and Mama planned on selling the fruit and vegetables at a nearby lumber camp.

After lunch, Mama put Ana and Rozalia down for a nap. Grandma Terezi was going to look after them. Then she wound a towel around her head to help support her basket of produce.

"May I please go with you?" Vladimir begged. While he didn't mind helping out Mama, he really just wanted to have some fun at the lumber camp with his friends.

"Fine," Mama responded. "Run and get another basket. We'll fill it with some more fruit and vegetables."

It wasn't the first time that Vladimir had accompanied Mama on the long and hilly trek to the lumber camp. Just to see all the men in action with their saws and other tools made carrying the heavy basket for the five-kilometer walk well worth the effort.

Vladimir anticipated meeting up with some friends from school. He also hoped to see the man who had made "klumpes" for him. Klumpes were wooden clog shoes that were stuffed with straw and worn just for fun. In the wintertime, he could convert the klumpes into skates if he was fortunate enough to find some wire to nail to the bottom of them.

As Vladimir and Mama neared the lumber camp, they saw a few other women with baskets of produce balanced on their heads. The workers at the lumber camp were accustomed to seeing the women vendors. At the end of their workdays, the men often bought produce to take home with them.

Vladimir spotted several of his school friends from Golenić. He handed Mama his basket of fruit and vegetables and then darted off towards them. The boys spent the afternoon running and chasing each other, pausing at times to watch the lumber camp workers as they chopped down trees and sawed off the branches.

It was fascinating for the boys to watch the workers as they loaded logs onto a railroad handcar. Resembling a miniature train car with wheels, the wooden handcar was used for transporting the logs out of the woods. Vladimir and the boys planned on using the handcar to push each other back and forth along the railroad track as soon as the men were done using it.

A group of Serbian boys from Lukovac must have had the same idea. When the handcar was finally free, both groups of boys reached it at about the same time. It didn't take long before there was a shouting match between the two groups.

"It's ours!"

"We had it first!"

"Get lost!"

Instead of compromising, the boys ended up in a fist fight, but Mama quickly ended the dispute. They had a fair distance to walk home, and she and Vladimir would have to hurry if they wanted to get there before dark. Thankfully they had sold almost all of the produce, and the near-empty baskets gave them a much lighter load to carry back to Golenić.

* * * * * * * * * * * * * * * * * * *

EDITOR NOTE: Whether at school or at the lumber camp, the children seemed to take sides according to their nationality. These childish quarrels were common, and it seemed to echo the tense conditions of world affairs. Adult life was primarily filled with friendly interactions and useful tasks, but if a disagreement arose, it didn't take long for the adults to also "take sides" based on their nationality. Just as the Yugoslavian villages exhibited their ethnic divisions, countries were also aligning between the Allies and the Axis Powers. Yugoslavia had joined the Axis powers on March 25, 1941.

(http://timelines.ws/countries/YUGOSLAVIA.HTML)

5

Changes
Spring 1941 – 1943

E veryone feared the inevitable signs of another war. Even children could sense the evil surrounding them. German warplanes flying overhead in the sky became commonplace for Vladimir and his classmates as they walked to and from school each day. Then word spread that German troops captured Belgrade, Yugoslavia. On April 17, 1941, Yugoslavia surrendered to Germany.

* * * * * * * * * * * * * * * * * * *

As is common with all families, the Fortnbahers also experienced changes over time . . . a new life born, and an old life expired. Grandfather Karlo's health had progressively declined. He passed away in 1942, the same year that Maritza, Vladimir's youngest sister, was born.

The scenes and rituals that took place following Grandfather Karlo's death could not easily escape from Vladimir's mind. Grandfather's mouth was wide open when he had died, and Mama tried so hard to close his upper and lower jaws together but she just couldn't do it. Tata built a wooden box for a casket.

Family and neighbors came to the house to give their condolences and to view Grandfather Karlo's body. The priest gave the funeral service and then demanded payment immediately afterwards. In the funeral procession that followed, two boys held crosses in front of the casket while four other boys served as pallbearers.

Even though Grandfather Karlo's death was traumatic to Vladimir, the experiences were eased by the warmth and love of family and by the knowledge that old age and death were natural occurrences of life.   Vladimir had looked up to Grandfather Karlo, and he would miss hearing his stories about being a soldier in WWI.

* * * * * * * * * * * * * * * * * * *

The political unrest occurring in their region seemed even more troubling than the death of a family member. Communist guerrillas arrived in Golenić. They were part of Tito's regime—a group referred to as "Partisans," and they had come to fight the Germans. The hilly and forested landscape surrounding Golenić offered a perfect hideout for them.

The leader of one of the Partisan units sought out Tata because he was the mayor of Golenić, and he ordered him to serve as their primary supplier. It was clear to Tata that he could either do as they demanded, or die. If the Partisans needed any information, or if they required supplies for their operation, Tata was expected to comply.

For an entire year the nerve-wracking, complicated process continued. Tata had to relay messages to the aggressive and radical Partisans in their region. At times he was also ordered to collect various food supplies such as deer meat and bread—mostly from the Golenić villagers, but sometimes even from some of the neighboring villages. As a twelve-year-old, Vladimir found himself caught in the middle. Tata sometimes used him as a messenger boy to notify neighbors of meeting times.

* * * * * * * * * * * * * * * * * * *

26

EDITOR NOTE: The Partisan army was a resistance movement in Yugoslavia that was led by Communist Josef Tito. The Partisans used hidden sabotage and other guerrilla tactics. By September 1941, it is estimated that there were about 70,000 resistance fighters in Yugoslavia.

(www.historylearningsite.co.uk/resistance_movement_in_yugoslavi.htm).

SECTION TWO:

World War II

6

The Evacuation of Golenić
Fall 1943 – Spring 1944

Vladimir's sleep was interrupted by some dogs barking uncontrollably during the night. He heard guns firing, followed by loud explosions. From the window he could see bright flashes of light. It appeared as though fire was erupting right out of the night sky.

The sounds of warfare had indeed become more and more common. It wasn't the first time that Vladimir had heard guns being fired or bombs exploding. The difference tonight was that the blasts were as loud as thunder, and the brightness of the fiery sky made him feel like he was in the middle of a battleground.

Then, in the midst of the explosions, there was a sharp knock on their door. When Tata opened it, there stood a few gruff-looking Partisans demanding more food and supplies. Through the jumble of voices Vladimir overheard that the village to the south of them had just been bombed. Once again Tata and the four other men assigned to him would need to impose on their neighbors in order to meet the demands of the guerillas.

* * * * * * * * * * * * * * * * * * *

A Golenić council meeting passed a vote that the villagers should join Tito's Partisan army to fight against the Germans. The news was relayed to the military commander of the Croatian army that was stationed in Podravska Slatina. The commander sent one of his units to Golenić to assist families

31

who wanted to leave the area so they could avoid having to serve in the Communist army.

"Whoever wants to flee may come with us to Podravska Slatina. Otherwise, you'll be forced to join the Partisans," the Croatian soldiers announced to the Golenić villagers.

"Let's go," Mama pleaded with Tata. "If we stay here, we'll be in the middle of the fighting." Tata hesitated, but Mama persisted with her appeal. "We won't be treated well by Tito's group because our last name is German," she said.

Many families from Golenić made a collaborative decision to leave, including the Fortnbaher family. Adults began packing their wagons with essential belongings while Vladimir and the other young boys and girls rounded up the large animals. Soon a long wagon train formed. Grandmother Terezi was not planning on joining them. She chose to stay behind on the farm.

There was quite a commotion at the start of the wagon train journey to Podravska Slatina. A woman, one of the Fortnbaher's neighbors, was desperately crying out for help because she couldn't hang onto the reins of her wild horses. Tata quickly handed Lisa and Sova's reins to thirteen-year-old Vladimir so he could help her gain control over the horses. The woman's husband was not with her because he had already fled from the region. Many of the men and older teenage boys from Golenić feared being captured and forced to join Tito's Partisan group.

The woman's horses continued to be restless and jumpy, so Tata drove her team of horses. He left Vladimir in charge of Lisa and Sova. Vladimir also had to take care of little Rozalia and baby Maritza because Mama, Dragutin, and Ana were with a group of adults and older children who were at the back of the wagon train herding the cows and pigs.

Rozalia held baby Maritza on her lap as she sat on the wagon seat next to Vladimir. One time the wiggly baby nearly fell overboard! It was a close call! If Vladimir hadn't grabbed her as quickly as he did, baby Maritza would have been crushed underneath the wagon wheels.

When the wagon train finally arrived at the stockyard within the city limits of Podravska Slatina, camp was set up. Each family found an area to park their wagon and hitch up their horses. Livestock that had been brought along on the journey from Golenić was sold to the Podravska Slatina residents for very low prices. The refugees from the wagon train wouldn't be able to maintain the animals for long, and so their only choice was to sell them. The primary goal was to save as much money as they could for future use, and to find enough food to survive.

* * * * * * * * * * * * * * * * * * *

While waiting it out in Podravska Slatina, the refugees occasionally left the city and returned to their farms in Golenić to get hay for the horses or to collect more belongings or food supplies for their families. The Croatian army escorted them on these 15-kilometer treks to and from Golenić to protect them from the Communist guerrillas, the Partisans. Mama and Dragutin took one of these dangerous journeys back to Golenić to get hay and food supplies because it was just too risky for Tata to go. Tata would be one of the first to be recognized and then forced to join the Partisans. Even worse, he could be killed.

When Mama and Dragutin reached their farm in Golenić, they found a very fearful Grandma Terezi. She explained that after the villagers had evacuated, the Partisans returned. Grandma Terezi said that the men were absolutely livid when they discovered that Tata had left.

"Where is Franjo? Why did he betray us? He was on our side!" The Partisans screamed at poor old Grandma Terezi and swore repeatedly. They emptied drawers and cupboards, and confiscated anything of value that they could find. In their raging madness, they smashed out the windows on their way out.

Tensions between the Croatians and the Communist guerillas had reached its peak in the Golenić area after it was discovered that the Croatian army had shot and killed a Partisan. Mama and Dragutin had persuaded Grandma Terezi to go back to Podravska Slatina with them. They also brought back hay for the horses, as well as the ducks, geese, and chickens that had been left behind when they had initially fled Golenić.

After three months of camping in the stockyard of Podravska Slatina, winter was approaching. The Golenić refugee families would need to find shelter for several months with the residents of Podravska Slatina. Tata knew a man in the city who was a Jehovah's Witness. He had occasionally stopped by at their farm back in Golenić. They had been on good terms with each other, and Tata had even received a Bible from him.

The Jehovah's Witness man welcomed the Fortnbaher family into his home, but his wife worried that the five children might turn her house upside down. Tata assured her that he was a strict disciplinarian, and all of the children proved his statement true by being well-behaved. The Fortnbahers lived there from January to April.

* * * * * * * * * * * * * * * * * * *

EDITOR NOTE: Some of the Golenić families had initially wavered in their decision to go to Podravska Slatina, but then finally decided to escape as well. Those families took up the tail end of the wagon train; however, a fair distance separated them from the large group of wagons and animals that were escorted by the Croatian army. Because they didn't have the same protection as the initial wagon train, the Partisans had caught up with them. They were stripped of their possessions and whipped.

* * * * * * * * * * * * * * * * * * *

EDITOR NOTE: Many of the Serbians sided with Tito, and the Croatians generally supported the Axis Powers. The Fortnbaher family was among those who were neutral. They made decisions based on personal safety, and simply wanted the conflicts to end without having to side with either political group.

7

Moving On
April – October 1944

T he Croatian army worked hard to protect the Podravska Slatina residents and Golenić refugees who had fled there, but the fighting between ethnic groups all around them continued. When a unit of the German army passed through the city, they offered assistance to civilians who wanted to travel with them. The Fortnbahers were among the families who began preparations to form another wagon train to leave Podravska Slatina.

Travelling with an army was necessary for protection. Although seldom seen, guerrillas were often present in the woods and they even hid themselves in fields. The German army was on guard, always prepared for conflict or battle.

* * * * * * * * * * * * * * * * * * *

Whenever the German army made a stop, the refugees did too, and their first stop was the small town of Donji Miholjac. The Fortnbaher family spent the night in one of the houses there. As Vladimir tried to get comfortable on a pile of straw in the front room, he could see that it would be nearly impossible to get a good night's sleep. A few German soldiers had set their machine guns through holes in the walls. During the night, the soldiers took turns between guarding and sleeping.

The German army and refugees stayed in Donji Miholjac for several weeks before the army decided to move on again. They planned for the refugee children and elderly adults to take a train to Sremska, Mitrovica while the rest of the adults followed with their horses, wagons, and livestock. The German army would lead the way in front of the train to check for mines or any other troubles. Eventually, the families would meet each other in Sremska, Mitrovica.

Vladimir, Dragutin, Ana, Rozalia, Maritza, and Grandma Terezi all boarded an open cattle train. On the first night, a heavy rain poured down on them. The children were cold and wet, and their hungry growling stomachs just added to their miseries. For three days and three nights the train moved slowly along the tracks. Thankfully, as their train passed through one of the villages, some kind people brought tea and food to them.

When the train finally arrived in Sremska, Mitrovica, the refugee children and elderly adults were taken to an arena. A humanitarian aid organization provided meals for them. It also helped the elderly adults watch over the children and hoped to reconnect them with their parents.

* * * * * * * * * * * * * * * * * * *

Many days passed before Vladimir heard the rumor that the adults who had followed behind the train would soon be arriving in the city! Vladimir quickly headed out to the main street to watch for any sign of Tata or Mama. Would they come today? What if he missed seeing them, or what if he'd never see them again?

Vladimir stood at the side of the road for endless hours, and he could hardly contain his anxiety. Finally, when he was sure that he had spotted Tata and Mama in the distance, Vladimir shouted and ran towards them. Tata and Mama were leading their horses and cow. Lisa and Sova were pulling the wagon with their belongings behind them. It really was a miracle! How the three of them cried, tears of happiness streaming down their cheeks as they embraced each other.

"Where are the others? Is everyone okay?" Mama was the first one to speak, but both she and Tata were utterly exhausted from the many miles they had journeyed. Vladimir assured them that the rest of the family was safe at the arena with Grandma Terezi.

Tata found a homeowner on the outskirts of Sremska, Mitrovica who let them settle their animals into one of his stalls. Then Tata and Mama collapsed from exhaustion on a pile of straw in the corner of the barn. Vladimir lay down beside them, happy and relieved.

When the man of the house came into the barn to feed his horses the next morning, he was surprised to find Vladimir and his parents sleeping there. "Ach," he exclaimed, "Why did you sleep out here in the barn? There was room in my house! I thought you had gone on to another house to sleep."

Tata, Mama, and Vladimir thanked the man for his kindness and then headed to the arena to join the rest of the family. How thankful everyone was to be together again! In the meantime, the refugee families had registered themselves at the city hall. Assignments were made for them to stay with individual families in the area.

Unfortunately the refugees and the host families weren't always pleased with the living arrangements made by the city hall. The Fortnbaher family was sent to the home of a widow, Mrs. Singler. Vladimir and his family were clearly not welcomed there. "You gypsies!" she shouted at them. "What are you doing here? Go back to your homeland where you belong!" Her son-in-law agreed with her and they both stood their ground.

Tata was disgusted by their attitudes, and Mama feared them. Not knowing what else they could do, the Fortnbaher family headed back to the arena. They came across two armed German soldiers who were commissioned to protect civilians. After explaining their dilemma to them, the two soldiers escorted the Fortnbaher family back to Mrs. Singler's home and emphatically stated that the widow <u>must</u> keep them.

It was difficult living with a family who made it obvious that you were not welcome, but Vladimir and his family did their best to live as peaceably as they could. The horses and cow were kept in a shed at the back of the Singler property. On a daily basis, Tata and Mama had to concern themselves with finding enough food for their family and the animals.

* * * * * * * * * * * * * * * * * *

One beautiful warm day in September, Tata led Lisa and Sova to graze in a pasture on the outskirts of the city. An elderly Serbian man had brought his sheep to graze there as well, and he struck up a conversation with Tata. After visiting for awhile, the Serbian man offered Tata some whiskey as a sign of friendship.

Two young men appeared in their midst, and the Serbian man introduced them as his sons. Tata detected that they were really Communist guerrillas when he overheard one of them whispering in his father's ear, "We'll take him to fight with us." Tata suddenly felt chills running up and down his spine even though it was a sunny day.

Fortunately the young men's father was protective of his newfound friend. "Leave him alone," he argued. "He won't be any trouble."

That incident set Tata on edge. He had put himself in a vulnerable position to be captured and forced to fight for the Communist guerrillas. The young men eventually moved on, and Tata promptly took the horses back to the Singlers' place. From that day forward, it was clear to Tata that he must stay hidden from public view.

* * * * * * * * * * * * * * * * * *

The Fortnbahers lived with the Singlers for seven months before news spread to Sremska, Mitrovica that the dreaded Russian army was coming to help the Communist guerrillas. On October 27, Tata heard of an organized plan for refugees to flee to Austria by train.

Mama, Grandma Terezi, Vladimir, Dragutin, Ana, Rozalia, and Maritza joined the crowds who waited to board trains headed for Austria. They had no idea exactly where the train would take them. Their main concern was to get away before the Russians came. Tata stayed behind to bring the horses and wagon as well as their belongings. He would be part of a wagon train that planned on leaving the city a few days after their train had departed.

The refugee train moved slowly. There was no particular timetable, and the refugees had no choice but to make the best of their less-than-ideal situation. The train often made brief stops as it passed through villages. In Pećs, Hungary, the train remained on the tracks for a little over a week before continuing on.

Whenever the train came to a stop, Vladimir knew the routine. Mama would need some wood and stones to be gathered so she could build a fire. Then she and the children would scrounge the area for anything edible that could be put into a soup. Occasionally, Mama would get out their precious stash of pig lard and a few loaves of bread. Everyone had to be watchful for signs that the train was ready to move again. No one wanted to be left behind.

While going through Hungary, warplanes flew over them. When some bombs unexpectedly dropped from the plane, they made an emergency stop. The refugees ran from the train cars to get away from the nearby explosions. Vladimir grabbed Maritza's hand, and everyone tried to find a bush, rock, or anything to hide behind that might offer some kind of protection.

Eventually, when the bombing ceased, the refugees headed back onto the train. It was difficult to know what to expect from day to day. Everyone's nerves were frazzled. They just hoped that the train would take them to a peaceful place so that they could live a normal life.

8

Refugees in Austria
December 1944 – April 1945

The refugee train traveled on for several weeks before crossing into Austria. It passed through Pećs and Pechlarn, and then made a stop in Wizenburg for two days and a night. In Wizenburg, Mama registered the family at the city hall. The city hall made living arrangements for the refugees at various farms among the surrounding villages.

Then the train continued on to Petzenkirchen, the Austrian village where the Fortnbahers would find their temporary housing. Petzenkirchen was crowded with refugees. Vladimir and his family were assigned living quarters on the second floor of an old three-story house. Prior to their arrival, the building had been used as a school for kindergarteners. The house sat on a hill overlooking an orchard.

Vladimir, Dragutin, Ana, and Rozalia attended the local school. Although it was a privilege for them to be able to continue their education, the language was definitely a barrier. Now they had to learn to speak and write German! What a blessing it was for Vladimir to discover that the teacher was fluent in Hungarian, too.

* * * * * * * * * * * * * * * * * *

Just before Christmas, news spread that a wagon train was headed towards Petzenkirchen. Mama and Grandma Terezi took turns standing by the roadside, hoping desperately to find Tata among the people passing through the village. After school, even Vladimir and Dragutin would take their turns watching. It was indeed a full-time job. They simply couldn't risk Tata walking right by them because they failed even a few minutes of their watching duties.

After days of constant watching, a wagon train finally began making its way through Petzenkirchen. It was chaotic; wagons, animals, and people were everywhere. Up until now there were no signs of Tata, but Mama spotted a woman who looked familiar. It turned out to be Mrs. Singler, the widow whose house they had stayed at while living in Sremska, Mitrovica. Apparently she, too, was now a refugee. When Mrs. Singler was within earshot, Mama just couldn't resist blurting out, "Now you can see how we had it!"

The days turned into weeks. Mama feared that they may have missed seeing Tata as he passed through Petzenkirchen, or that he'd taken another route. But since they couldn't be sure of anything, they all continued taking their turns watching out for him.

It was Mama who finally caught sight of Tata late in the evening on the following day. What a miracle! With the lack of communication, not all families were as fortunate to find each other.

Tata had left Mitrovica with the wagon train only a few days after Mama and the others had departed by train. He described his journey of enduring chilling winds and even some snow drifts along the way. Tata wasn't properly dressed for such a trip, and altogether it had taken about six weeks before he finally made it to Austria.

* * * * * * * * * * * * * * * * * * * *

The Austrian government did their best to help out the refugees by giving them ration cards. Unfortunately, they weren't enough to feed families. Sometimes Vladimir's sisters even went begging for food throughout the village of Petzenkirchen so that the family would have enough food to eat.

At this point in time, Tata was left with no other choice but to sell their horses. Vladimir felt extremely crushed. To be without horses? Lisa and Sova had been with his family for as long as he could remember. So many memories of the horses they had on their farm back in Golenić flooded his mind—from seeing the young foals at the moment of birth, to bringing them treats and riding them around in the pasture.

Tata found a local farmer that needed a team of horses to deliver his milk. He bought Lisa and Sova for a fair price. Vladimir and Dragutin were elated every time they saw "their horses" on the milk route!

* * * * * * * * * * * * * * * * * * *

In Petzenkirchen, it didn't take long for Tata to find a job working for the mayor. His other workers were French prisoners of war. Since Tata couldn't speak French, the men had to communicate to each other with hand motions. The job didn't pay much, but it did help supplement the meager portions of food that they received with their ration cards.

While living in Petzenkirchen, warplanes flew overhead on almost a daily basis. Bombs had already dropped on nearby villages like Amsteten. Whenever Vladimir or his family heard the sound of planes, they would instinctively run outside and hide themselves among the trees in the orchard by the hillside. They sure didn't want to risk being buried alive under an old building!

Vladimir once witnessed a chain bombing that was way too close for comfort. His whole being had shaken with fear as he watched the explosions from the orchard. He could only imagine the destruction that the bombs had caused.

* * * * * * * * * * * * * * * * * * *

By April the Russian troops drew close enough to Petzenkirchen that Tata felt the need to once again move the family to a safer location. This time there was no organized plan for the refugees. Each family had to fend for themselves. The Fortnbahers packed up their clothing and cooking utensils and headed out to the roadside to decide where their next move would be. Before long a German army truck passed by them, and Tata pleaded with them to take the family to the train station at Pechlarn.

The German army truck did take them as far as Pechlarn. At the train station, Tata discovered a freight train that had stopped briefly to refuel. It was headed towards the American-controlled region of Austria. Since it appeared that the more peaceful Austrian region would be the safest move for them, Tata inquired about the possibility of their family being able to ride along on the freight train.

Tata was given permission for the family to board the train, but they had to share a train car with another refugee family. The freight train didn't have any seats so they made makeshift seats with their luggage. That night everyone tried to find space among the luggage for some much-needed sleep.

The freight train stopped in Salzburg for several days. While in Salzburg, American warplanes suddenly appeared in the sky. Everyone in sight ran to a nearby field, where they were instructed to lay flat and remain still until the warplanes finally left the area.

Another time, the bomb sirens rang. This was a warning to seek cover immediately at the nearest bomb shelter. Fourteen-year-old Vladimir hurriedly ran along with the rest of the crowd. By the time he reached one of the shelters, Vladimir realized that he was no longer with any members of his family. Alone with strangers, he squeezed into the underground shelter. Where were his parents and his siblings? Weren't they right behind him? Was it possible that they had run to a different shelter?

"Move on back! Move on back!" a police officer hollered to the frightened crowd.

Vladimir crouched down. He was pressed by people on all sides of him as they attempted to make room for those still outside. Meanwhile, Vladimir worried about his family. When the raid was finally over, would he be able to find them? What if they hadn't even made it to a shelter?

Eventually the air cleared and the people were released. Vladimir was grateful to finally get out of the cramped space and take in some breaths of fresh air. As he made his way back to the freight train, his feelings of fear turned into joy when he caught a glimpse of Tata, Mama, and the others. The rest of the family had ended up in a different bomb shelter than Vladimir, and they too had been anxious about their separation.

* * * * * * * * * * * * * * * * * *

By May 1945, the train moved on again, this time heading towards the Austrian province of Tyrol. It traveled slowly, and stopped often. There was simply no hurry in going to an unspecified destination. The train ride consisted of watching the landscape and looking out for anything edible along the way. Bathing was a rare luxury.

When the train arrived in the village of Leogang, it stopped right in the middle of the tracks for three weeks straight! Then it continued to make its way along the railway tracks. It was late spring by the time the train reached the picturesque town of Zell am See, Austria, and it was here that Vladimir saw the first signs of American troops.

Vladimir and Dragutin admired the clear blue-green lake that was visible from where they stood by the railway. They spotted several boys swimming in the lake, and soon they joined them in the cool refreshing water. Vladimir was still wet when he got back onto the freight train. Some of the men on board were shouting excitedly about the rumor spread by the American soldiers that **the war was now over!**

* * * * * * * * * * * * * * * * * * *

EDITOR NOTE: At some point while Vladimir and his family were living in Austria, his father changed their last name from Fortnbaher to Fortenbacher. The spelling of Vladimir's name was also changed—from Vladimir to Wladimir, and his brother's and sisters' names were changed as well. The rest of the story will reflect the new last name change, but the first names will remain the same to prevent confusion.

Fortenbacher family photo taken in Salzburg, Austria, 1945
L – R: Tata, Ana, Rozalia, Vladimir, Dragutin, Maritza, Mama

9

American Soldiers
Summer 1945 – Summer 1946

After several days in Zell am See, the freight train moved on again to the Austrian village of Kaprun. There Tata found a small wooden barrack that would serve as the family home for the summer of 1945. The Fortenbachers soon learned that the "end of the war" did not mean the end of their struggle to survive.

Tata and Vladimir both found jobs in Kaprun doing "dirt work" with a group of other refugees. Even though Vladimir was old enough to work, his frame was weak and frail from the lack of nutrition. The men's job was to hand-shovel the earth to prepare the groundwork for an electrical plant that would be built on the site. The best part, of course, was going back to the barrack at the end of the day and eating Mama's hearty potato soup. Potatoes were their primary food source.

By the end of the summer, the refugees at Kaprun were told that they needed to move on again. The Fortenbachers and some other refugee families loaded their belongings onto a train which took them as far as Salzburg. The refugees were able to stay in a horse arena that had previously been used as a veterinary hospital for wounded horses.

Soon the American army invaded Austria and overtook the weakened German army. The American soliders distributed food supplies to the refugees, and they tried to keep them busy with odd jobs. Unfortunately, it wasn't long before it became apparent that the army needed the space in the arena that was occupied by the refugees. All of the refugees were once again forced to move on.

48

The family moved into a government building in Ridenburg, a small suburb of Salzburg. The building was crowded with refugees, and they had to share one room with several other families. Beds were stacked up against the sides of the walls in order to make room for everyone. Eventually word spread that the refugees could move back into the horse arena.

Vladimir and his family remained at the horse arena until June 1946. The United Nations set up a soup kitchen there, but the small portions that they handed out were never enough to fill the boys' bellies. Occasionally Vladimir joined some boys who went to the American army kitchen to beg for leftovers. At best, an American soldier would hand them a plate of nearly consumed food to lick clean.

Vladimir was quite intrigued by the American army camp. One day he climbed a fence and watched intently as two workers unloaded bread from a truck. One of the men took notice of Vladimir looking at them through the wire fence. "Toss me your cap, boy," he shouted to Vladimir.

From where Vladimir was standing, he couldn't make out what the man said to him, but it didn't take him long to figure out his hand motions. Vladimir threw his cap towards the man. He filled Vladimir's cap full of bread crumbs before handing it back to him. The thoughtful gesture had made his day—what a treat!

* * * * * * * * * * * * * * * * * * *

The local American army division gave the refugees some jobs. It was a good thing because it helped Vladimir stay out of trouble. His first job was to clean the bathrooms and shower rooms within the army camp. He gave all of the money that he earned to his parents to help support the family.

Vladimir befriended a refugee boy who worked with him in the army camp. His friend's curiosity had gotten the best of him one day as they passed the supply room. He coaxed Vladimir to go inside with him to look through the numerous bags and boxes. "Think we'll find any good pocket knives?" his friend said.

"We're sure to find some useful things," Vladimir replied.

The two young boys began snooping through the American army supplies. Suddenly Vladimir heard a man shouting, and then the door behind him slammed shut. His friend was nowhere in sight. He must have made his escape through the maze of supplies. Vladimir cowered as an American soldier yelled harsh-sounding phrases at him in a language that he didn't understand.

The American soldier led a shamefaced Vladimir into a nearby jeep. They drove in silence to another army building. Once inside, the soldier marched him into a room that looked like an office. By now Vladimir was in tears, and he shook with fear over what they would do to him. Soon two other American soldiers came into the office. One of them must have been an interpreter. He asked Vladimir some personal questions in Hungarian, and then he and the other soldier disappeared.

It seemed like an eternity before Mama showed up at the office with the interpreter and the other American soldier. Mama was made aware of the boys' mischievous incident, and of how Vladimir had been caught trespassing within the camp.

Mama privately questioned Vladimir, and then turned to speak with the interpreter. "He was with a friend," she said. "It was his friend's idea to snoop through your supplies, and Vladimir went along with him." The interpreter and the other American soldiers had some further discussions. It was finally decided that the army would release Vladimir back to the refugee camp. How thankful and relieved Vladimir felt for the mercy that was shown to him!

* * * * * * * * * * * * * * * * * *

50

One day Vladimir was asked to help unload some boxes and bags of supplies from train cars. He watched how the strong American soldiers lifted up bags and then organized them into a pile. It seemed easy enough for him to do.

Vladimir reached into the train car and grabbed one of the bags . . . Ouch! A sharp pain tore up his back. He couldn't think for a moment, and then he stumbled away from the train car. Unfortunately his tall, lanky, and malnourished body wasn't able to support heavy weight like the hefty American soldiers' bodies could. Vladimir was in so much pain that he couldn't even stand back up, so he crawled back to the refugee camp on his hands and knees.

* * * * * * * * * * * * * * * * * * * *

Tata found a new job working at a castle in Salzburg. The American army general for the 42nd division lived at the castle. He employed several men, including Tata, to do maintenance work inside the castle. One of his fellow workers there told him about an apprentice program for young men.

"Vladimir, I heard that there's a trade school close by for those age fifteen and older," Tata told him that evening. "I think you should do it. Learning a trade will help you get a good job."

After making some inquiries, Tata sent Vladimir to the trade school, where he found an apprentice job with a tailor. One of his first lessons was to make buttonholes. Again, all of the money that he earned was given to his parents. Not only was it customary, but the rationale was that single people didn't need any money. Vladimir didn't really enjoy his apprenticeship, but he felt it was important to be able to contribute to his family's well-being.

Evenings were anything but dull for the refugee boys. The boys played soccer in a field close to the refugee camp. Sometimes they would go fishing at the lake, and since there never seemed to be enough food, Vladimir's family appreciated any fish that he or Dragutin caught.

In the evenings, the children would also scavenge through the army garbage bins. Sometimes they found perfectly good shirts that only had small stains on them. Vladimir and the refugee boys also found treasures that were not very beneficial for them, such as half-smoked cigarette butts. The boys liked to smoke, and they were baffled as to why the soldiers were so wasteful in throwing out half-smoked cigarettes.

* * * * * * * * * * * * * * * * * *

One evening, when Tata arrived back from working at the castle, he had a co-worker with him. As Tata introduced the man to Mama, he added, "John and I have been talking at work. He wanted to meet the family." The man shook hands with Mama and seemed to be at ease in their modest makeshift home in the corner of the arena.

During dinner the adults discussed political matters. Then the visitor switched the conversation to another topic. Vladimir listened as the man spoke of his faith in Jesus Christ. He described his Christian conversion and baptism in the Nazarean Church, and pointed out the Bible's plan of salvation for all who were willing to receive it. Vladimir could tell that the man's faith was very important to him.

When the man left, Mama sighed. The conversation had disturbed her. "Why did he need to tell us about such things?" she stated. "We're fine just the way we are."

"Now, Katarina," Tata replied calmly, "What he says makes sense. I'd like to learn more about it."

"You know what the neighbors will think," Mama continued. "They won't want a thing to do with his religion, and I sure don't want him coming back either. There's no need for more religion around here."

Photo taken while living in the Austrian barracks
Top Row: Mama and Grandmother Terezi
Bottom Row: Maritza, Rozalia, Ana, Dragutin, and Vladimir

10

The Nazarean Church
1946 – 1947

"**K**atarina, I think we should move to Wels," Tata announced one evening. "I heard that there are a lot of jobs there because of the destruction from the bombings."

"Where will we live?" Mama wondered.

"There's a large refugee camp there, too" replied Tata. "We'll more than likely meet others from the Golenić area."

Mama smiled at that.

"I'll find out when we can get on the next train," Tata said quickly, before she had a chance to change her mind.

The moving process was relatively simple because there wasn't much to move. Wels was filled with refugees, and it proved to be even more industrious than they had hoped for. Tata, Vladimir, and even Dragutin quickly found jobs. As Tata had predicted, they did meet old acquaintances from Golenić. Vladimir reunited with some of his former friends, and he continued with the typical teenage social activities of dancing and going to shows.

In Wels, Tata made a new friend, Mr. Wechter. Mr. Wechter did not smoke or drink as many of the other men did, and he reminded Tata of John, his old friend from Salzburg. He invited Tata to attend a service at his church. Tata said that he was not surprised to learn that he, like John, was from the Nazarean church. There was something about the Nazarean faith that intrigued Tata even though the rest of the family was not interested.

Although the move to Wels appeared to be a progressive step, the winter of 1946–1947 was very difficult. Sadly, Grandma Terezi passed away. Food and clothing were in short supply despite Tata, Vladimir, and Dragutin holding down jobs doing mechanical and construction work. The girls did what they could to help out, but they weren't old enough to get jobs.

* * * * * * * * * * * * * * * * * *

One cold winter day, Mama asked Ana to go to local farms and beg for eggs. Ana despised begging but she knew that it was the only way she could contribute to the family's needs. She obediently put on her threadbare coat and then draped Rozalia's small coat over her shoulders to protect herself from the bitter winds. In her previous begging encounters she had found a couple of farm families who had consistently shown her compassion.

Ana hurried as fast as she could. She didn't need to explain that she was from the refugee camp because it was obvious from the way she looked. Ana was relieved when she was able to bring home some eggs, the very thing that Mama had hoped for. Next time it would be Rozalia's turn to go begging.

When Tata came home that evening, he was happy to find that there was a hot meal waiting for him. The inside of the barrack was nearly as cold as the outside, and some warmth in the stomach would help. "That smells like—" Tata's words were cut short by a coughing fit.

Mama looked concerned. "Your cold doesn't seem to be getting any better," she said. "If anything, it's gotten worse."

Tata shrugged. He stomped his feet and rubbed his reddened hands together, trying to coax a bit of warmth into them, when he had another coughing attack. The tattered coat, multiple layers of threadbare shirts, and worn-out socks and shoes were not sufficient to keep out the cold during his long days at work.

After eating, Vladimir overheard Tata speaking with Mama. "Katarina, I've been going to church alone for quite some time. I would like you to come with me." Mama didn't argue, and Tata continued, ". . . and the children."

* * * * * * * * * * * * * * * * * * *

The Fortenbaher family began attending weekly Sunday services at the Nazarean Church. Vladimir listened to the sermons as the minister spoke about Jesus Christ, the Son of God, who had been born of a virgin. He preached about how Jesus lived a sinless life before dying a terrible death on the cross, and that His precious blood was shed for the sins of the world. "Today is another day of grace," the minister said.

Vladimir found himself caught between two worlds. On Saturday nights he attended ungodly activities with the other refugee teenagers. Then, on Sundays, he attended church with his family and was exposed to the biblical teachings from the Holy Bible. This struggle between the two ways of living continued for about a year.

In the meantime, Tata's chronic coughing persisted. It worsened to the point that there was no other option but to admit him to the hospital. The rest of the family continued to attend church on Sundays.

Vladimir noticed that the young adults of the Nazarean Church were different. When they sang beautiful hymns, passion seemed to flow right out of their hearts. They had a genuine joy about them that was missing from his life.

As Vladimir began paying more attention to the sermons, he realized that true happiness did not come from living in "pleasures of the moment." The conviction of the Holy Spirit weighed heavily upon him, and he surrendered his heart in humble repentance. God's grace was sufficient to help Vladimir seek God's will for his life.

It was not surprising that Vladimir's friends and coworkers didn't understand the sudden change in his life. "Vladimir," they teased, "Why would you hang out with all those old mourners from church when you could be having the time of your life with us?"

Vladimir found comfort in the Bible verses, "For the time past of our life may suffice us to have wrought the will of the Gentiles, when we walked in lasciviousness, lusts, excess of wine, revellings, banquetings, and abominable idolatries: Wherein they think it strange that ye run not with them to the same excess of riot, speaking evil of you" (1 Peter 4:3–4) KJV.

As the oldest among his siblings, Vladimir was burdened by the responsibility of his family. Tata was in the hospital and it was difficult trying to make ends meet. Despite these trials, Vladimir felt God's peace in his heart as he lived out his faith. What an encouragement it was when Mama also experienced a spiritual conversion!

* * * * * * * * * * * * * * * * * * *

EDITOR NOTE: The origin of the Nazarean Church dates back to Switzerland in the 1830s. Samuel Heinrich Froehlich (1803–1857) completed seminary training and began his ministry in the Protestant state church on May 27, 1827. Samuel was removed from the state church in 1831 because he would not adhere to some of their teachings. For example, he was convinced that infant baptism was not according to the Bible.

(Ruegger)

As an evangelist, Samuel Froehlich took several missionary journeys throughout Switzerland. He endured hardships and opposition from the state church along the way.

By 1836, fourteen churches in Switzerland were founded under his leadership. These churches became known as Evangelical Baptists. Congregations formed in Germany, Austria, Hungary, and the Balkan region, including Bosnia, Serbia, and Romania. The Eastern European churches became known as Nazareans. According to acc-nazarean.org, it is estimated that, even before WWI, there were about 30,000 Nazareans in Hungary alone.

(Ruegger)

The first North American church was founded in Croghan, New York in 1847. As more Evangelical Baptists and Nazareans began immigrating to North America, significant church growth took place in the Midwest region of the United States. The North American churches adopted the name Apostolic Christian. Some North American churches became divided because of language and cultural traditions. This resulted in the Apostolic Church branching out into two church divisions: the Apostolic Christian Church of America, and the Apostolic Christian Church (Nazarean).

(http://www.acc-Nazarean.org/Church%20History/church-history-5.html)

To this day, some of the Apostolic Christian (Nazarean) churches still retain some of their European customs, and sermons are preached in both English and native languages. Apostolic Christian Churches of America and Apostolic Christian Churches (Nazarean) are located in many states within the United States, as well as Europe, Canada, Mexico, and Japan. Mission outreaches exist on every continent.

(http://www.acc-Nazarean.org/Church%20History/church-history-5.html)
(http://apostolicchristian.org/about_origin.php.)

SECTION THREE:

Changes

11

Baptism
August 1947

On Friday afternoon, August 29, 1947, a large group of Nazareans gathered in Braunau, Austria for a very special occasion. Forty-three individuals, including Mama and seventeen-year-old Vladimir, were prepared to share their testimonies of faith and get baptized. Tata was not with them because he was still hospitalized in Wells.

Nazarean families and friends had come not only from the village of Braunau, but also from surrounding villages by buses and trains. In order to accommodate the large crowd of people, an old inn had been rented for the weekend church services. One by one, the 43 individuals took turns giving their personal testimonies of how God had forgiven their sins and changed the desire of their hearts to live for Him. Each one expressed their faith in Jesus Christ and professed that they were at peace with God and man.

By late Friday evening, there were many more individuals who had not yet given their testimonies. The plan was to continue hearing the testimonies on Saturday morning from where they had left off. Local villagers returned to their homes for the night while the visitors remained at the inn. Care packages that included blankets and food were provided by the local brethren. When it appeared that there weren't quite enough blankets to go around, some of the group decided to take turns sleeping. A number of people sang hymns for awhile, and then later switched places to sleep while others sang. Everyone had a chance to sleep, and the night passed by quickly.

On Saturday morning the testimonies continued all day long until the sun was beginning to set. After the last individual's testimony was heard, the entire group of people walked the short distance from the inn to the bank of a nearby river. Willow trees at the river's edge whispered softly in the humid air. Everyone stood quietly, and Vladimir couldn't imagine anything more serene.

The song leader gave a pitch, and then the voices of those assembled gave praise to the Lord for His goodness and provision. A beautiful melody of sopranos, altos, tenors, and basses harmonized perfectly over the still waters. Even amidst poverty, homelessness, and difficult circumstances, there was much thankfulness and joy among the group.

Vladimir, Mama, and the other 41 individuals lined up to be baptized in the river. All of them made a covenant to stay true and faithful to God all the days of their lives. After the baptism, the congregation sang "The Baptismal Covenant" from their hymnal. The church elder completed the baptismal service with a prayer for the Holy Spirit's guidance over each one of the 43 individuals as they continued their life in Christ.

Again, the local villagers returned to their homes for the night, while the visitors remained at the inn to sleep. On Sunday morning benches were set up inside the inn for a regular church service. The sermon seemed especially powerful to Vladimir that morning, and the encouraging words would provide an extra measure of strength in the days and weeks that followed. Communion was served following the church service.

The weekend had been full of fellowship and singing. The people were physically tired, but spiritually refreshed. Many of the visitors needed to be back to work on Monday morning, and they had many hours of traveling before them. The group parted ways after wishing each other God's blessings.

* * * * * * * * * * * * * * * * * *

EDITOR NOTE: *It is ironic that Braunau is the city of Hitler's physical birth and Vladimir's spiritual one.*

12

Immigrating
1948 – 1955

Tata remained in the hospital in Wells, and his health was progressively declining. Vladimir was very concerned about Tata. It was Tata who had initially started going to church, and he had been the one who encouraged Mama and the rest of the family to go as well. Yet, within his own life, there appeared to be an obstacle in the way of submitting his life to the Lord.

In 1949, Tata was diagnosed with tuberculosis. He was transferred to a hospital in Berg, Austria where he underwent lung surgery. Lying in a hospital bed day after day, Tata struggled not only with his physical illness, but also with his lost eternal state. It was only by God's grace that he was finally able to turn to the Lord in repentance. Because of Tata's debilitating condition, he was baptized in his hospital bed.

Tata began making small strides of improvement in his health condition. However, the family worried about what they would do once Tata was released from the hospital. He would still require lots of medical attention, and he wouldn't be able to live in the poor and crowded conditions at the refugee camp. Their future looked bleak, and so Vladimir and his family prayed about their next move.

For the past six years the Fortenbacher family had been refugees in Austria. They had no intention of returning to their homeland in Yugoslavia where there was always fighting between the ethnic groups, so they began the process of immigrating to another country. America was their first choice, followed by several other European countries. But because of Tata's poor health, their application to America was denied.

64

* *

It was at least a year and a half before Tata was finally discharged from the hospital. The lung surgery had left him in a much weakened state. But the family's hopes soared when their immigration applications had been accepted in both Sweden and Norway!

In the fall of 1951, the Fortenbacher family took a train to Oslo, Norway, and then to their final destination of Utøy Inderøy, located close to the city of Trondhaim. There, they were assigned to live with a farm family. Tata was too weak to do any work, but Vladimir and Dragutin were able to find jobs. Mama helped the farm family as much as she could. Ana and Rozalia worked as household maids, and Maritza attended school.

Vladimir worked for a fisherman in the neighboring village of Stromen making wooden fishing boxes. He lived with the fisherman during the week, and returned to the farm with his family on the weekends. While working alongside the fisherman, Vladimir began to learn the Norwegian language. The Fortenbachers stayed with the farm family for about six months before moving on to live with another Norwegian farm family in Utøy Inderøy.

In 1952, Vladimir worked at a tool and die company in Kirkneswogen. At this point in time, the Fortenbacher family had lived in Norway just over a year. Tata's health had improved significantly during that time, and the family still hoped to immigrate to America.

Unfortunately, the quota of people accepted to America was already met, so Vladimir's family decided to fill out an application for Canada instead. As part of the application process, the Canadian government required immigrant families to have a sponsor. Acquaintances John and Julia Stemler from Windsor, Ontario agreed to sponsor the Fortenbacher family.

Vladimir, Dragutin, and Rozalia were the first members of the Fortenbacher family to receive acceptance papers to immigrate to Canada. The entire family moved to Drammen, a Norwegian port city. They found space to live in a YMCA among other immigrant families. Three passenger tickets were obtained for *Stavanger Fjord*, a steamship that would take Vladimir, Dragutin, and Rozalia across the Atlantic Ocean. Tata, Mama, Ana and her husband Zivoin Ivkovic, and Maritza planned on living at the YMCA while they waited patiently for their acceptance papers.

* * * * * * * * * * * * * * * * * * *

On June 6, 1955, Vladimir, Dragutin, and Rozalia traveled by train to Stavanger. In the harbor, the three siblings joined the hundreds of immigrants who boarded *Stavanger Fjord*. The old Norwegian steamship made its way across the sea to Copenhagen, Denmark to pick up more passengers. Then it crisscrossed back to the Norwegian harbor of Bergen for the remaining passengers. The ship was very crowded.

Vladimir had mentally prepared himself for rough seas as the *Stavanger Fjord* began to make the long voyage across the Atlantic Ocean to Canada. Their sleeping quarters were on the lowest deck, and in an area of the steamship that had a sickening odor of oil. But other than a bout of nausea, it turned out to be a rather smooth trip. During the two-week journey, Vladimir overheard the sailors talk of how they usually had to tie down the chairs and tables during mealtimes.

On June 18, the *Stavanger Fjord* arrived at a port in Halifax, Nova Scotia. Vladimir, Dragutin, and Rozalia held on to their small pieces of luggage as they joined other immigrants walking across the ship's gangplank to face their new world. A majority of the passengers remained on the ship, which would continue on to the New York harbor.

Photo of Fortenbacher Family while living in Norway
L-R: Rozalia, Ana, Mama, Maritza, Tata,
Vladimir, and Dragutin

Photo of Vladimir, age 23, in Norway

Photo of Vladimir's Norwegian Passport

13

Settling in Canada
1955

T he three Fortenbacher siblings found themselves in the midst of a land that appeared strange and exciting at the same time. Their knowledge of Hungarian, Serbian, Croatian, German and Norwegian did not help them here in Canada. It was confusing because everyone around them spoke in different languages. Signs and printed materials were also completely foreign looking.

Vladimir stared at the automobiles whizzing past them. He had seen cars before, but never this many. The automobiles here were much larger, and they came in so many different colors! But the three of them were not in Halifax, Nova Scotia to simply stand and gawk at their surroundings. There was an important task in front of them—finding the train station where they could buy tickets with the paperwork the Canadian government had given them. Their intended destination was Windsor, Ontario. It was there that they hoped to find their immigration sponsors, the Stemlers.

Vladimir, Dragutin, and Rozalia boarded a westbound train. They were very hungry by the time the train made a brief stop in the province of Quebec. Vladimir wanted to purchase coffee and donuts for the three of them. Since he couldn't make out any of the conversations around him, he had to use hand motions to communicate. Adding to the confusion was the fact that the people from Quebec spoke both French <u>and</u> English.

On June 21, 1955, Vladimir, Dragutin, and Rozalia finally arrived at John and Julia Stemler's doorstep, where they were warmly welcomed in. Since the house next door was unoccupied at that time, the three of them were able to stay there temporarily. Vladimir gave thanks to the Lord for their safe journey to Canada, and prayed that the rest of the family could soon join them.

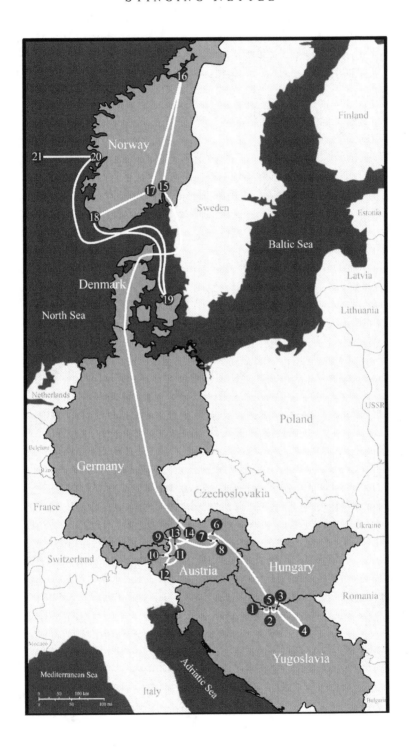

Vladimir's Journey
from Birthplace to Arrival in Canada

1. Golenić, Yugoslavia
2. Podravska Slatina, Yugoslavia
3. Donji Miholjac, Yugoslavia
4. Sremska Mitrovica, Yugoslavia
5. Pećs, Hungary
6. Pechlarn, Austria
7. Wizenburg, Austria
8. Petzenkirchen, Austria
9. Salzburg, Austria
10. Leogang, Austria
11. Zell am See, Austria
12. Kaprun, Austria
13. Salzburg, Austria
14. Wels, Austria
15. Oslo, Norway
16. Utøy Inderøy, Norway
17. Drammen, Norway
18. Stavenger, Norway
19. Copenhagen, Denmark
20. Bergen, Norway
21. Halifax, Nova Scotia, Canada

PART II
Margaretha's Story

Table of Contents

Introduction to Margaretha's Story

Margaretha Wittmann's story begins with a childhood experience she had at approximately three years old. She doesn't clearly remember it happening, but her parents had reminded her about the event many times as she was growing up. She and her siblings called their father "Tate" (pronounced tah-teh), and they called their mother "Mame" (pronounced mah-meh). Margaretha's story is more difficult to follow than Vladimir's because of the many relatives that are so interconnected with her WWII experiences.

The Wittmann and Deschner families originated from Germany. In the mid to late 1700s, German farmers and tradesmen were encouraged to migrate to central Europe to develop the vast amount of uncultivated land. Settling all along the Danube River plains in Austria, Hungary, Yugoslavia and Romania, these German pioneers became known as the Danube Swabians, who acquired their own unique culture and distinctive German dialect. Margaretha's ancestors moved to Yugoslavia (present-day Serbia), and established the village of Neu Pasua. Farming was the primary way of life for the Neu Pasuans, and they were known for their orderliness and work ethic.

In the Neu Pasuan village it was rather confusing because every family named their children by the same traditional names. The oldest son was named after his father, and it wasn't uncommon for one of the daughters to have the same name as her mother. Margaretha has three aunts and five cousins who are also named Margaretha. Fortunately the narrative includes only three other Margaretha's: an aunt, a cousin, and an older woman named Margaretha who was a relative of her uncle.

While growing up, Margaretha was nicknamed "Gretle" (pronounced grade-leh). "Gretle" is used throughout the book when Margaretha's family members or relatives are addressing her. The endearing nickname is still used by her close friends and family.

In Margaretha's story, asterisks are used within chapters to note a change of event or gap in time. Editor's notes are included at the end of some chapters to give the reader clarification or insight about some of the events that take place.

The map below shows the Danube River, which begins in Ulm, Germany and flows throughout Europe.

(Danube-research.com/map)

Wittmann Genealogy

Jakob Wittmann (1875) & Florina Schreiber (1876)

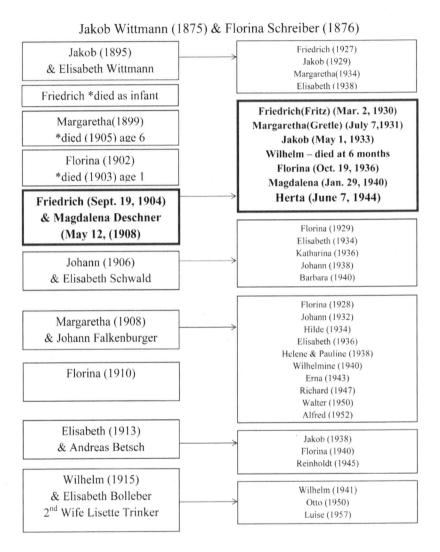

Jakob (1895)
& Elisabeth Wittmann

→ Friedrich (1927)
Jakob (1929)
Margaretha(1934)
Elisabeth (1938)

Friedrich *died as infant

Margaretha(1899)
*died (1905) age 6

Florina (1902)
*died (1903) age 1

**Friedrich (Sept. 19, 1904)
& Magdalena Deschner
(May 12, (1908)**

→ **Friedrich(Fritz) (Mar. 2, 1930)
Margaretha(Gretle) (July 7,1931)
Jakob (May 1, 1933)
Wilhelm – died at 6 months
Florina (Oct. 19, 1936)
Magdalena (Jan. 29, 1940)
Herta (June 7, 1944)**

Johann (1906)
& Elisabeth Schwald

→ Florina (1929)
Elisabeth (1934)
Katharina (1936)
Johann (1938)
Barbara (1940)

Margaretha (1908)
& Johann Falkenburger

→ Florina (1928)
Johann (1932)
Hilde (1934)
Elisabeth (1936)
Helene & Pauline (1938)
Wilhelmine (1940)
Erna (1943)
Richard (1947)
Walter (1950)
Alfred (1952)

Florina (1910)

Elisabeth (1913)
& Andreas Betsch

→ Jakob (1938)
Florina (1940)
Reinholdt (1945)

Wilhelm (1915)
& Elisabeth Bolleber
2nd Wife Lisette Trinker

→ Wilhelm (1941)
Otto (1950)
Luise (1957)

80

Deschner Genealogy

Wilhelm Deschner (1880) & Margaretha (Hartman)

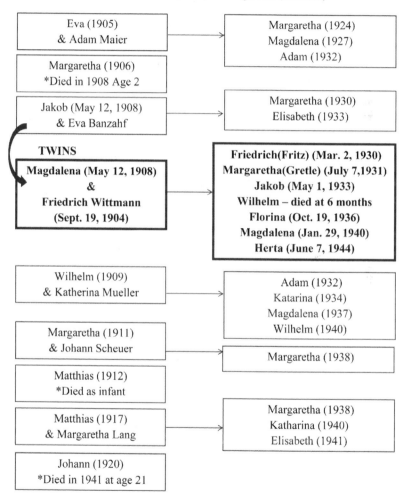

Eva (1905)
& Adam Maier

→ Margaretha (1924)
Magdalena (1927)
Adam (1932)

Margaretha (1906)
*Died in 1908 Age 2

Jakob (May 12, 1908)
& Eva Banzahf

→ Margaretha (1930)
Elisabeth (1933)

TWINS

**Magdalena (May 12, 1908)
&
Friedrich Wittmann
(Sept. 19, 1904)**

→ **Friedrich(Fritz) (Mar. 2, 1930)
Margaretha(Gretle) (July 7,1931)
Jakob (May 1, 1933)
Wilhelm – died at 6 months
Florina (Oct. 19, 1936)
Magdalena (Jan. 29, 1940)
Herta (June 7, 1944)**

Wilhelm (1909)
& Katherina Mueller

→ Adam (1932)
Katarina (1934)
Magdalena (1937)
Wilhelm (1940)

Margaretha (1911)
& Johann Scheuer

→ Margaretha (1938)

Matthias (1912)
*Died as infant

Matthias (1917)
& Margaretha Lang

→ Margaretha (1938)
Katharina (1940)
Elisabeth (1941)

Johann (1920)
*Died in 1941 at age 21

SECTION ONE:

Margaretha's Early Years

1

Neu Pasua
1934

Three-year-old Margaretha was with Tate at the neighbor's house when a wagonload of grapes had just been brought back to their Neu Pasuan village. Margaretha's uncles had been busy gathering grapes in the vineyards several kilometers away in the highlands. The Danube region's large grapes were like no others—deep purple and white varieties that were bursting with sweetness and flavor!

Margaretha was an inquisitive child who loved being in the middle of any exciting happening. After Tate teasingly motioned for her to run home ahead of him, Margaretha ran as fast as she could before she realized that something was not right . . . perhaps she had already passed her house on Obergassee Street! Suddenly the lines of houses, strips of fences, and tidy yards all looked exactly alike. How would she ever find her way?

New Pasua was a close-knit community where neighbors looked out for each other. Two of the village girls could tell that Margaretha was hopelessly lost, so they brought her to the city hall. There they found the trommler who served as the town crier.

The trommler knew most of the village folks because of his weekly Saturday afternoon news rounds. He took one glance at Margaretha's frightened face between the two young girls and said, "Oh, I know which family she belongs to. She is the Wittmann's Gretle!" Soon Margaretha was delivered safely home. What a relief to reach their yard gate and run into the house!

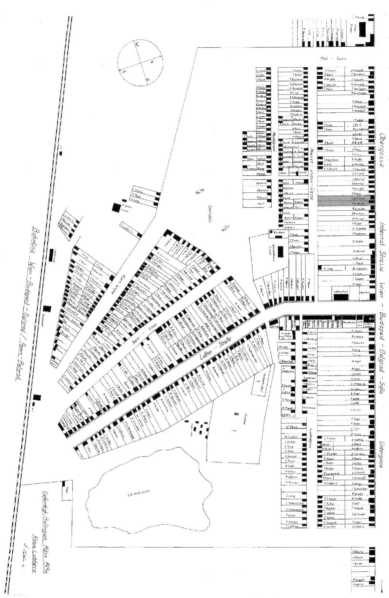

Map of Neu Pasua, Yugoslavia.
Margaretha's property is highlighted.

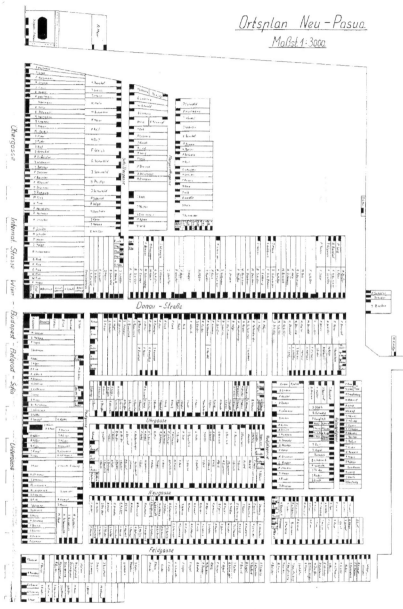

From *Neu Pasua Heimatbuch* (Hudjetz-Loeber)
The village name has since been changed to
Nova Pazova, Serbia.

Besides Tate and Mame, Margaretha's family included her older brother Friedrich Jr. (Fritz), and her younger brother Jakob. Martin, the hired hand, and Katarina, the maid, were much-appreciated additions to the Wittmann household. Martin was a conscientious worker, but kept mostly to himself. He slept in a loft above the horse stall. Katarina's duties made her more closely connected with the children. Her bedroom was next to Margaretha's.

* * * * * * * * * * * * * * * * * * * *

Farmers in Neu Pasua worked from morning 'til night during the planting season. Then, beginning with the barley harvest in June, there was hardly a break from the endless fieldwork tasks. Tate and his hired hand Martin spent long days in July harvesting their wheat. Because Tate owned one of the few threshing machines in Neu Pasua, he hired three men to take his threshing machine from farm to farm to harvest for anyone who hired them. Tate would oversee their jobs, but he was usually kept occupied with his own abundance of field work.

Corn shelling was one of the most backbreaking tasks, but fortunately it was also one of the last responsibilities for the harvest season. Many extra hands were needed because the corn was removed from the cobs by hand! There were no machines to do the work, and so Tata hired five to six laborers every day until the work was completed.

During corn-shelling season, Mame and Katarina were kept very busy preparing meals for the family and the work crew. Mame also took food to a sickly woman who lived across the street from them. The widow didn't have any children or relatives to help her, and so Mame did what she could to look out for her.

In November, butchering days would begin with the poignant smell of garlic being cleaned, and end with delicious meals of Metzelsuppe, pork, bread, fried potatoes, cracklings, cake, and doughnuts. Aunt Eva, Mame's older sister, was the master soapmaker on butchering days. Only winter gave enough time for leisurely activities such as festivals and knitting parties.

* * * * * * * * * * * * * * * * * *

EDITOR NOTE: Neu Pasua was founded in 1791 by 62 German pioneer families. When Margaretha was a child, the village had grown to over 6,000 residents who lived along the 21 streets. Each lot was a half yolk deep, and the houses were positioned close to the streets. Many lots also included a smaller house which served as a starter home for a young couple. The farming land was beyond the outskirts of the village.

(Hudjetz-Loeber)

The Neu Pasuan villagers were independent from their German homeland, and they lived peaceably among the Yugoslavian citizens. Neu Pasua was a self-sufficient village that comprised of many tradesmen such as blacksmiths, wagonmakers, tailors, and clockmakers, and industries such as a brickyard, oil mill, and two large flour mills owned by the Binder and Gerber families. The village had over a dozen grocery stores, inns, and even a cinema. Most Neu Pasuans never left their village, and if they did, it was only to visit a neighboring village.

(Hudjetz-Loeber)

* * * * * * * * * * * * * * * * * *

EDITOR NOTE: As you will note from the Wittmann geneology, Margaretha has three uncles and three aunts. Her uncles and their wives and families also lived in Neu Pasua. The Wittmann families were closeknit, and they worked together through the harvest and during butchering days. Grandfather and Grandmother Wittmann lived fairly close to Margaretha's family. After midweek market days, Grandfather looked forward to "coffee" at his house to discuss farming plans with his three sons.

Margaretha's Aunt Margaretha was the first one of the Wittmanns to move away from Neu Pasua. She married Johann Falkenburger from the village of Franztahl. Located about 15 kilometers from Neu Pasua, Franztahl was a village of mixed German and Serbian ethnicity. In those horse-and-buggy days travel was difficult, and visits to Franztahl were seldom. Every year Grandfather made a special trip there to help them during butchering days.

Aunt Florina Wittman was still single when Aunt Elisabeth got married to Andreas Betsch and moved to his village of Beška. Beška was approximately 10 kilometers from Neu Pasua and the villagers were also of German and Serbian ethnicity. Aunt Florina moved to Beška after Grandfather Wittmann bought a large farm there and divided it between his two daughters. Margaretha has fond memories of taking the train to Beška with her cousin Liese and spending a whole summer at Aunt Florina's house.

* * * * * * * * * * * * * * * * * * *

EDITOR NOTE: Margaretha's mother Magdalena Deschner was one of six children. The Deschners also resided in Neu Pasua. Although the Deschners were not as financially well off as the Wittmanns, they were known by their friendly personalities. Eva was the oldest of the Deschner children followed by the twins Magdalena (Mame) and Jakob. Next in line came Wilhelm, Mattias, and then Johann.

Mame had just finished the 5th grade when Grandmother Deschner died while giving birth to Johann, who was born deaf and dumb. She was left in charge of raising her younger *brothers with Eva's help before her older sister got married. Matthias was just a two-year-old at the time of their mother's death, and he and Mame had developed a special closeness. Grandfather Deschner was tall and muscular. Whereever he went throughout Neu Pasua, Johann was always seen at his side.*

2

Baby Wilhelm
1936

The long winter days passed, and by early March, Tate and Martin were busy plowing and harrowing for another planting season. Springtime also brought on more responsibilities for the womenfolk of the village. Houses were thoroughly cleaned and whitewashed inside and out. Vegetable and flower gardens were planted. Cooking, baking, and laundry were among the neverending jobs.

Only six months ago, baby Wilhelm had become the newest member of the Wittmann family. Tate had hired another maid in addition to Katarina to assist Mame with her extra workload. But tonight, Mame had more on her mind than her daily household chores. Baby Wilhelm had a fever, and she just couldn't seem to get him settled.

Mame prayed fervently. She could tell that baby Wilhelm was seriously ill. She rocked and cooed and sang softly to comfort him. The Wittmanns had not yet lost a child to the "deadly fever," but many Neu Pasuan families had lost a small child in these same circumstances.

Mame kissed Wilhelm's hot cheek and said another prayer. She continued her vigil over the baby, but his illness worsened. The fever spiked and the doctor was summoned.

"Our baby boy is very sick." Tate's voice was serious as he greeted the doctor at the door.

When the doctor entered the house, Tate quickly led him towards the chair where Mame was holding Wilhelm, who was pale and limp. Margaretha had tiptoed behind the kitchen counter to hide. But when the doctor gently laid Wilhelm on the pillow that was placed on the table, Margaretha peeked out from her hiding spot. The doctor pulled a needle out of his black leather bag. Perhaps it would help. How she desperately hoped for baby Wilhelm to get better!

* * * * * * * * * * * * * * * * * *

Baby Wilhelm just couldn't recover from the deadly fever. His little soul went to be with Jesus in heaven. Margaretha heard the three successive and monotonous tones of the church bells ring, announcing to the entire village that someone under the age of twelve had died. That evening the relatives gathered to mourn with them, and the pallbearers brought the coffin into the house.

The funeral followed the traditions of the village, from the pallbearers nailing down the coffin and carrying it on a brier, to the choirmaster leading the funeral hymns. Margaretha had dressed in her Sunday petticoats and dark woolen skirt.

* * * * * * * * * * * * * * * * * *

On October 19, Tate took five-year-old Margaretha, six-year-old Fritz, and three-year-old Jakob outside to assist him with yardwork. All morning long he had them busily digging in flower beds and other such tasks. At noon, Tate directed their attention towards the house. He announced, "Come see what the stork has brought us!"

The excited Wittmann children ran into the house. Katarina led them into Tate and Mame's bedroom. There, wrapped up in a blanket in Mame's arms, was the most beautiful baby girl that Margaretha had ever seen! How tiny her hands and feet were—and what a funny cry! Margaretha examined her over and over again. Her own little baby sister— it was hard to believe that she was real.

Tate and Mame named the baby Florina. Every day after school, Margaretha was anxious to get home so she could hold the baby and play "house" with Jakob.

3

Sundays
1940

Mame gently shook nine-year-old Margaretha out of her deep sleep. "Gretle, time to be up and dressed!" As Margaretha lay in bed for a few moments of extra sleep, she sensed that it was not a typical school day. Today, of course, was Sunday.

Before getting ready for church on Sunday mornings, Mame routinely set out the homemade noodles and started a pot of soup on the stove for the noon meal. Margaretha attended early service at the Nazarean Church with Mame while Tate stayed home with the boys and little Florina. He also maintained the woodstove, and kept an eye on the simmering soup. Tate rarely attended church.

Mame was baptized in the Nazarean Church in 1935. Her baptism did not follow the tradition of her Lutheran parents. Instead it followed in the ways of her maternal grandparents and in-laws. Grandmother Deschner had died while giving birth when Mame was only twelve years old. That left Mame with a lot of responsibility in caring for baby Johann and her two-year-old brother Mathias. It was from her Grandmother Deschner's respect for the Nazareans that encouraged Mame to also seek out that faith.

* * * * * * * * * * * * * * * * *

After lunch, Tate and Mame had their weekly ritual—a quick nap! At 1:00 p.m., Margaretha, Fritz, Jakob, and the other Neu Pasuan children went to the Lutheran Church Sunday school for Bible lessons. They were often given a plaque with a Bible verse on it to memorize.

There was an expectation for all of the school-aged children in Neu Pasua to go to the Lutheran Sunday School. On Monday mornings, the teacher frequently asked her students to raise their hands if they had attended Sunday school that week. Even though Margaretha enjoyed going to the Nazarean Church with Mame, she also went to the Lutheran Sunday School to avoid being teased.

* * * * * * * * * * * * * * * * * * *

EDITOR NOTE: The Neu Pasuans didn't work on the Lord's Day. They did only the necessary tasks of preparing meals or feeding their livestock. All of the Neu Pasuan villagers were Lutheran, except for a small percentage of them who were from the Nazarean faith. Even the school was operated by the Lutheran Church. The Nazareans had different religious viewpoints from the Lutherans, and they also refrained from taking part in the village festivals. In such a tight-knit community that followed age-old traditions and religious teachings, it was not looked upon favorably to be different.

4

School Days
1940

"Gretle, Gretle! Get up! You don't want to be late for school!" Mame's voice was insistent, and it stirred Margaretha out of her deep slumber.

"Oh, why do school mornings have to come around so early?" Margaretha thought. She hurriedly put on her white, long-sleeved blouse underneath her blue-patterned dress. The apron-like bodice of her dress had two ties that crossed over her back and fastened to buttons on the back of her wide pleated skirt. Mame helped pin her two thick braids around the top of her head.

After eating a quick breakfast of Cream of Wheat, Margaretha picked up her leather school bag and ran to catch up with Fritz. Her tall and lanky brother was good-natured. He always seemed to be singing or whistling a tune as he went about his business around the farm. Away from the farm, though, Fritz was quiet. Margaretha was just the opposite. She liked to be in the middle of the action surrounded by her school friends.

At school Margaretha headed to her all-girl, 2nd grade classroom. Boys and girls were separated in grades one through five, but in the 6th grade boys and girls were combined. Since books were quite limited, most of the school lessons revolved around memory work. Margaretha used a small piece of chalkboard to neatly copy the long quotes on the board and to work out her math problems.

When Margaretha finished her copy work, she noticed that her friend Katherine Maier had also completed her work. "Psst . . ." she whispered. Katherine turned to look, and soon the girlish gossiping began.

"Katherine! Gretle!" The teacher's sharp voice demanded their attention. With approximately 700 children in the village school, there was no tolerance for foolishness and wasting time. "Come here," the teacher commanded as she pointed her ruler to the front of the class.

With eyes glued to the floor and hearts pounding, the girls obediently made their way towards the teacher. Their upturned hands felt the sharp sting of the ruler before the girls shamefully returned to their seats.

* * * * * * * * * * * * * * * * * * *

One winter day after school, Margaretha went sledding with a group of children. Neu Pasua consisted mainly of flat farmland, but some boys had scooped up enough snow to form a small hill. The children used their leather school bags for makeshift sleds.

Margaretha was so caught up with the thrill of sledding that she did not pay attention to her inadequate outerwear. Soon her hands and feet were numbed from the bitter chill in the air. Nothing seemed to stop her—not even the other children picking up their school bags one by one and walking home.

After many more sled rides, Margaretha decided that she should probably go home too. When she got to the bottom of the hill, she reached down to pull out her school bag . . . she was too tired and frozen to move! She glanced around helplessly. The other children were nowhere in sight. She slapped her stiff legs with her numb hands, but they wouldn't budge. Margaretha lay panic-stricken in a heap at the bottom of the hill.

It was Mr. Kniesel who noticed Margaretha lying in the snow on his walk home from the train station. The Kniesel family lived in the Wittmann's smaller house on their property, and their oldest child Laura was Margaretha's age. When Mr. Kniesel realized that she was so frozen that she couldn't even stand up, he picked her up and carried her home.

Mame's voice was faint. "Ach, that Gretle! She enjoys her fun!" Those were the last words Margaretha remembered hearing before she drifted off to sleep.

* * * * * * * * * * * * * * * * * * *

On January 29, 1940, another little baby sister, Magdalena, was born. Magdalena was a darling baby with dark hair and large brown eyes. Cousin Elisabeth often came over to hold the baby and to spend time with Margaretha.

Cousin Elisabeth, nicknamed Liese, was from the Wittmann side of the family. She was close to Margaretha's age, and the two of them grew to become inseparable friends. Margaretha and Liese loved biking together after school. They shared one bike; each girl rode on opposite sides. In a standing position, the girls placed both feet on their own bike pedal as they leaned towards each other against the bar between the bike seat and handle bars. Their outside arm grasped the handle bar while their inside arm clutched around the other girl's waist to prevent from getting thrown off balance. Oh, how much fun and laughter they'd have together as they rode up and down the streets of Neu Pasua!

* * * * * * * * * * * * * * * * * * *

EDITOR NOTE: The village bells gave a sense of order to the day for the Neu Pasuan residents. The community sexton rang the bells at 7:45 a.m. to warn children to depart for school, once at noon and again at 1:45 p.m. to remind children to head back to school from their lunch break at home. The sexton also took care of the Lutheran Church property, but his most important task was in being punctual in the manual chore of ringing the village bells.

(Hudjetz-Loeber)

Neu Pausans valued children and large families were considered a sign of being blessed and prosperous. In 1931, the year that Margaretha was born, Neu Pasua had registered 134 births. This resulted in very large classrooms.

(Hudjetz-Loeber)

5

The Knitting Party
1940

The day was filled with a frenzy of cleaning the parlor and making preparations for the knitting party. Tonight's party was at the Wittman home and would be hosted by their maid Katarina. Margaretha followed Katarina up into the attic to get several bunches of dried corn cobs. Together they carefully removed the corn kernels from the cobs to make popcorn for the evening snack.

Excitement was in the air as the guests began to arrive. As usual, the young women arrived first. They found a comfortable chair and promptly started on their needlework. Before the young men were expected to arrive, Katarina took Margaretha aside and whispered, "Gretle, do you want to hide above the doorway?" The rest of the young women giggled, knowing exactly what the scheme would entail.

The Wittmann house had a rounded window that was above the porch entrance. The thick sturdy door frame provided a ledge large enough for a small child to sit on. Margaretha nodded her head, pleased to be in on the big girls' plan. "Now, when the first boy comes in," Katarina instructed, "reach down and snatch off his hat."

Margaretha sat giddy with anticipation, and tried hard to be patient. Oh, how she looked forward to playing a prank on an unsuspecting young man! However, the plan went awry when the first "young man" through the door happened to be none other than Mr. Friedrich Wittmann, Margaretha's Tate! He looked up and announced sternly, "Gretle, come down – now!" The young women blushed and looked away, unwilling to admit their participation in the scheme.

If it had been Fritz or Jakob, a spanking would have been in order. But it was different with Margaretha. She had learned to holler loud enough that her father would say, "Ach, that little Gretle, I never even touched her, and she cries as if I whipped her like a boy. Oh, what's the use?" Once again, Margaretha got away without punishment.

* * * * * * * * * * * * * * * * * * *

Whenever there was a knitting party in their home, Margaretha liked observing the young men as they put some beans or corn kernels into little matchboxes. The matchboxes would rattle as the men helped the women wind their wool around them.

During the knitting parties, the Wittmann children usually stayed out of the way by spending the evening in their parent's bedroom. Furnished with a couch and table and chairs, the bedroom almost resembled a living room. It was also one of the few rooms in the house that had its own woodstove for heat.

Margaretha enjoyed these cozy family times. Tonight she entertained the younger children by playing a homemade game that used beans and corn kernels for the playing pieces. Mame worked on some mending, and Tate read from the Bible before drifting off to sleep. All too soon Mame said, "Children, Tate's already sleeping. It's time for bed!"

Fritz complained about having to go to a cold bedroom, so Mame let them hold their blankets close to the wood stove until they were toasty warm. Then, very quickly, they dashed to their bedrooms before their blankets had a chance to get cold.

Margaretha went to sleep in Katarina's bed, but she didn't fall asleep right away. It wasn't the first time that Katarina had asked her if she wanted to sleep in her bed. Margaretha, of course, was always thrilled to be asked, even though she knew that Katarina would eventually carry her back into her own bed during the night. Apparently all she cared about was having her bed warmed.

Margaretha heard laughter as the young men and women were leaving the knitting party.   Then the laughter subsided, and a beautiful melody in mens' voices broke the silence. "It has been quite an adventurous day," Margaretha mused as the singing grew fainter.

* * * * * * * * * * * * * * * * * *

EDITOR NOTE: Knitting parties let single men meet young women. It also provided an opportunity for the women to complete items for their extensive dowries. (Hudjetz-Loeber)

Margaretha's parents, Friedrich Wittmann and Magdalena Deschner, first met each other at a knitting party. In 1928, Friedrich's younger brother Johann had returned home from army training and he was anxious to get married. However, it was against the custom for a younger brother to get married before the older one. Finally Johann had threatened, "Friedrich, if you don't soon find a girl to marry, I'll get married before you."

Friedrich's response was, "Be patient. I'll go out and find myself a woman, and then we can have a double wedding." Friedrich was already twenty-four years old. Young men in Neu Pasua were typically married between the ages of eighteen and twenty.

Being pressured by his younger brother, Friedrich attended a knitting party with a mission in mind. On the first evening he merely sought out Magdalena Deschner's eyes, which caused her to blush. Magdalena Deschner, at twenty years old, was also well past the usual marrying age of sixteen to seventeen for women.   After several more knitting parties, Friedrich finally found the courage to ask Magdalena to marry him.

Friedrich, however, was in a bind because he had been raised in the Nazarean Church during his childhood years. Magdalena was already confirmed in the Lutheran Church. In order to marry Magdalena, Friedrich would also have to get confirmed in the Lutheran Church. He decided to go through with the confirmation process, even though it caused him embarrassment because of his age.

Meanwhile Johann became engaged to Elisabeth Schwald, another Lutheran woman. Johann had attended the Lutheran Church with the other village children on Sunday afternoons and had secretly gotten confirmed when he was twelve years old, so it was not an issue for him. Three weeks after their engagements were announced in the Lutheran Church, the two couples were married on November 29, 1928.

Passport photo of Uncle Jakob Wittmann

Photo of Aunt Elisabeth, wife of Jakob Wittmann

Photo of Friedrich Wittmann (Tate)

Photo of Magdalena Deschner-Wittmann (Mame)

Photo of Uncle Johann Wittmann taken while serving in the
Yugoslavian army

Photo of the three Wittmann aunts:
Florina, Margaretha, and Elisabeth

Photo of Uncle Wilhelm Wittmann
pictured with his 2nd wife Lisette,
Cousin Willie (Wilhelm Jr.) and Otto

SECTION TWO:

World War II

6

Soldiers Arrive
1941

"Gretle, Florina, come quickly!" Jakob excitedly shouted out to them one spring day. "The army is coming!" Margaretha set one-year-old Magdalena down on the floor and hurried out the door with Florina. Katarina picked up Magdalena and curiously followed the girls outside. Jakob was right. The German army had indeed reached Neu Pasua.

Other neighbors joined them as they excitedly made their way to the street. Soon people were lined along both sides of Obergasse Street. Soldiers marched past them . . . . row after row of soldiers in green uniforms. Then tanks, trucks, and more soldiers—seemingly without end!

The Germans were invading Yugoslavia. With the threat from Serbs in the area, the village of Neu Pasua was elated to see soldiers of their own nationality. To them, the German uniforms symbolized safety.

It was just one week before Easter, and many housewives had already made Easter treats of cakes, bacon, and sausages. The villagers threw these treats to the soldiers as if they were in a parade. Eventually Margaretha grew tired of watching the soldiers and went indoors. All day long they continued to march—even throughout the night, and into the next day.

* * * * * * * * * * * * * * * * * *

A Volkswagon broke down and was pushed into the Wittmann's yard by the two German army soldiers who had

113

been riding in it. As Tate approached the two men, Margaretha and some of the other village children followed behind him. They tried to make sense of their conversation. What did it all mean? What would happen next?

In the following week, there was a sharp knock on the Wittmann family's front door. A soldier was standing on their porch and requested overnight accommodations. Apparently a unit of the German army was spending the night in Neu Pasua. Mama hurriedly made up a bed for him. He was gone by the next morning.

After that, the family grew accustomed to housing soldiers for brief overnight stays. War was brewing around them, but the bells still chimed daily throughout Neu Pasua. Life for the villagers continued rather normally with births and deaths, weddings and village traditions. Occasionally the childrens' education was interrupted when the army troops used their school building.

* * * * * * * * * * * * * * * * * *

Eleven-year-old Fritz detested the poems he had to memorize for school. He was often still working on the first stanza on the day before he was to recite it. Since memory work took little effort for Margaretha, Mame often petitioned her to help out. "Come on, Gretle," she said. "Help Fritz learn his poem."

Margaretha picked up Fritz's book and began instructing her older brother, "Repeat after me," she said. *"Es kracht der Schnee, der Wagen knarrt, Mit langen Zapfen steht und start."*

Fritz methodically repeated, "Es kracht der Schnee, der Wagen knarrt, Mit . . ."

"Es kracht der Shnee, der Wagen knarrt, Mit langen Zapfen steht und starrt," Margaretha said without even glancing down at the words. "Try it again, Fritz." And so it

was that soon Margaretha could recite the poem while Fritz was still struggling.

Fritz wandered outside to find Tate. There was always manure to pitch, and soon there would be more fieldwork that needed to be done. "School is just not for me," Fritz said to Tate. "I'm a good worker. Please let me stay home from school and help you. Then you won't need to look for hired hands anymore."

Unfortunately for Fritz, the village decided to offer an additional year of schooling while he was in the 5th grade. The students' education would now extend through the 6th grade. In the typical Neu Pasuan way, when something was initiated, the entire village was expected to conform.

Fritz was determined to stay away from school. Tate had to admit that it was difficult to find hired help because of all the young men being drafted into the German army. From that time forward, Tate allowed Fritz to skip school and help around the farm, even though they were likely to be fined by the school officials.

* * * * * * * * * * * * * * * * * * *

EDITOR NOTE: Yugoslavia joined the Axis powers on March 25, 1941. On April 13, 1941, Belgrade was captured by German troops, and then on April 17, 1941, Yugoslavia surrendered to Germany.

(http://timelines.ws/countries/YUGOSLAVIA.HTML)

Margaretha is the 2nd girl from the right. This photo was taken by a German soldier and later given to Margaretha.

7

Childhood Struggles
1942

U nderground bunkers were constructed within the Neu
Pasua region in the event of possible bombings. The
Wittmanns had a bunker built on their property
between the big and small house. Fritz and Jakob, however,
decided to use the bunker for another purpose. It became a
perfect hideout for their cigar-smoking experimentation. When
Tate caught them red-handed, he gave them the whipping that
they deserved.

In the meantime, Margaretha had her own issues. While
she was busy packing her leather school bag, Jakob walked past
her and teasingly gave her a punch in the shoulder. Margaretha
was in no mood for his immature behavior. "Mame," she cried,
"Jakob hit me again!"

But she knew what Mame's response would be: "Don't
hit him back or it will only make it worse. Just leave him be."

It was difficult to take Mame's advice and not retaliate.
Margaretha turned her thoughts to her school friends and the
fun times that they had at recess with jump rope and ball
juggling. Margaretha was pleased with her ability to juggle
three balls in the air, and four against the wall. She was now in
the 6th grade, her final school year.

* * * * * * * * * * * * * * * * *

During the next school day, Margaretha did her copy
work quickly and was the first one to be finished. She glanced
across the aisle at her friend Katherina. She couldn't help but

notice her pretty earrings. Oh, how she wanted earrings like the other girls!

Whenever Margaretha asked if she could get her ears pierced, Mame would remind her of the verse in the Bible from 1 Peter 3:3 that admonished against placing emphasis on outward adornment. No matter how much Margaretha whined and complained, she always got the same negative response. How she despised being so different from the Lutheran girls!

Margaretha's daydreaming was interrupted by the schoolmaster's voice. "Gretle, you may go help out with the Grade 1 students." (The 5th or 6th graders who had completed their work early were sometimes asked to help out with the younger students.)

Margaretha was assigned to a 1st grade boy. Every time the boy used his left hand for writing, Margaretha's job was to switch the pencil from his left hand to his right hand. It was a standard in Neu Pasua that all children must learn to write with their right hand. As the boy became increasingly frustrated, Margaretha empathized with him. Her own brother Jakob had the same struggle. He, too, was left-handed.

* * * * * * * * * * * * * * * * * *

Aunt Elisabeth stopped by with her three daughters Liese, Katarina, and Barbara. "Friedrich," she said to her brother-in-law. "I'm taking my girls to get their ears pierced. Why don't you let Gretle come with us?"

At first Tate was reluctant. Then he thought about how nice it would be to finally end Margaretha's whining and complaining. Besides, he didn't have any personal conviction against earrings. Much to Margaretha's delight, he gave his consent for her to go along with her aunt and cousins.

The girls giggled with excitement as they headed in the direction of the jewelry store. Once inside, the girls took turns sitting on a chair. Margaretha watched closely as a man cut a potato in half and held it behind cousin Katarina's ear. Then, with a quick poke, a golden earring was pressed in. Soon it was her turn . . . Ouch! It hurt a lot more than she had expected. All too quickly Aunt Elisabeth brought the girls back home again.

The breeze was blowing with a coolness that often comes before a storm. Soon the wind picked up and dark clouds gathered. Tate was frantically trying to get a wagonload of grain into the barn before the imminent downpour. He caught sight of Margaretha and called out, "Gretle, come quickly and help us!"

Margaretha hesitated; she had other things on her mind. Her hesitation, however, only intensified Tate's sense of urgency. Impatiently he shouted out to her, "Just because you got earrings doesn't mean you get out of doing work!" Margaretha knew that she didn't work as diligently as Fritz, but she didn't appreciate Tate's teasing about her earrings. She obediently went to help bring in the grain.

Jakob had overheard Tate's teasing, and was more than pleased to repeat the phrase as supper was being prepared. "Just because you got earrings doesn't mean you get out of doing work!" Margaretha glared at him angrily. To make matters even worse, even Stevo the recently hired Slovakian man chimed in.

After supper Margaretha wanted to nurse her sore ears, but a pile of dirty dishes was waiting. "Gretle, come help wash the dishes," Katarina called out to her. "Just because you got earrings doesn't mean you get out of doing work!"

Margaretha grew more frustrated than ever. With all the teasing around her, she wanted to tear out her beloved golden earrings. Mame was right—earrings didn't make her one bit happier!

Wittmann family photo taken approximately 1942
L – R: Fritz, Jakob, Tate, Mame, Magdalena (on lap),
Margaretha, and Florina (front)

8

More Signs of War
1943 – 1944

Tate was unusually quiet. Something was bothering him. "…. and she said that she was surprised to still see me around here," Margaretha overheard Tate complaining to Mame. "And she wondered why I was not serving in the army. She accused me of being a rich man who paid my way out!"

Margaretha knew that the neighbor woman took pleasure in giving Tate a hard time for not being off to war. "I told her" Tate continued, " 'For all the flack you ladies are giving me, there's no place I'd rather be!' " He grimaced as he attempted to straighten his right arm.

"Ach, Friedrich," Mame soothed. "Don't you worry. She misses her husband and sons who have had to leave home to serve in the army. The neighbor woman can say whatever she wants about you, but we know the truth and have nothing to hide."

Tate's bent arm didn't stop him from doing his regular work. He was fourteen years old when he had broken it. Since Neu Pasua didn't have a hospital, Grandfather Wittmann tried to set his arm as well as he could. When Tate turned eighteen, he had been drafted into the Yugoslavian army. However, he was soon dismissed because of his disability and labeled as "unfit". It was only when he rode a bike that Margaretha noticed how curved and awkward his arm looked.

In the meantime, Mame's stomach seemed to get bigger and bigger on a daily basis. On June 7, 1944, another little baby girl was added to the Wittmann family. Margaretha had wanted to name the baby "Elisabeth" after her cousin and best friend.

But that was not to be. When the midwife came to help deliver the baby, she brought a list of boy and girl names that parents could choose from. The list of names came from a decision made at the city hall. The council realized how much confusion there was with all of the villagers having similar names. Mame and Tate eventually decided to name the baby girl "Herta".

* * * * * * * * * * * * * * * * * *

The rumor about the German army invading their village turned out to be true. The army set up a base in Neu Pasua, and an airport was constructed on the outskirts of the village. Neu Pasua was only 18 kilometers from Belgrade, the capitol city of Yugoslavia. Many families were asked to host army officers in their homes.

The Wittmann family was assigned to keep the army's major, Erwin Menge. Major Menge slept in the spare bedroom. On their property he parked a camper, which served as his office. Inside the camper were a bed, a table, some chairs, and even a closet. Margaretha and Liese sometimes used the camper for a playhouse.

Major Menge was a tall, slim man, so contrary to Tate's muscular and broad-shouldered stature. Instead of eating at the army kitchen with the other soldiers, the major always showed up at the Wittmann house at meal time. He just couldn't say enough about Mame's fine cooking. During watermelon season, he seemingly got great satisfaction from cutting up the many juicy watermelons that were grown in their watermelon patch.

In the evenings, Major Menge spent time teaching Fritz how to play chess. It was Jakob, though, who quickly grasped the strategies of chess playing. Jakob was so different from Fritz. He excelled at school, but it was always a struggle to get him to do any physical work around the farm.

* * * * * * * * * * * * * * * * * * * *

The trommler brought some very disturbing news. He announced to the villagers that no one was allowed to patronize a particular textile store any more. The announcement was followed by a threat that, if they did, their picture would be taken and publicized. There were three textile stores in Neu Pasua, and the forbidden shop was owned by a Jewish family.

Despite the trommler's warning, Margaretha was with Mame one day when they had entered the forbidden shop. Margaretha was fearful that their picture would be taken, but Mame reassured her that there was no reason not to patronize this shop, and that the threat didn't scare her one bit. Margaretha hesitantly looked through the rows and rows of beautiful fabrics that were cut to order on two large tables in the middle of the shop. She was keenly aware that the two of them were the only customers in the shop that day.

A couple of weeks later, Margaretha and her siblings were locked in their parent's bedroom. They were instructed to play games. Margaretha didn't know why they had to stay in Mame and Tate's bedroom for the day, but it was later rumored that the Jewish family was taken away to the village of Zemun. They were never seen again, and the shop had been completely emptied.

* * * * * * * * * * * * * * * * * * * *

EDITOR NOTE: Was it possible that Margaretha's parents were trying to protect their children from being exposed to potential violence? Who was behind the eviction of the Jewish family? Margaretha never heard her parents discussing the incident, and so she never really knew what had happened that day. The empty textile shop was later used by the Neu Pasuan women and girls to braid wet straw to make boot coverings for the German army.

9

Fleeing Day
October 6, 1944

E arly in the day on October 5, 1944, thirteen-year-old Margaretha saw the trommler making his way down Obergasse Street. Anxious to hear the latest news, the Neu Pasuan residents headed to the street and crowded around him. "Tomorrow at 1:00 p.m.," he solemnly announced, "everyone must be ready to leave. The Russians are coming!" The German army was in trouble, and it was imperative that the villagers flee before their enemy arrived.

The news was not entirely unexpected. Just last week the German residents of the neighboring village of Franztahl had to flee, and they all passed through Neu Pasua with a wagon train on their way to Austria. Tate, Mame, Margaretha, and Fritz had run out to meet Uncle Johann and Aunt Margaretha Falkenburger with seven of their children as a horse pulled their wagon through the village.

The trommler moved on to spread the sobering news. As the Wittmann family headed back inside their home that morning, they did not resume their normal activities. Everyone turned their attention to the important task of packing. Clothes, bedding, and dishes were packed along with anything else that could fit into their wagon.

Up until now the villagers had continued in their daily routine despite the threat of war. But in an instant that threat knocked directly on their doors. The villagers' sleep that night was anything but peaceful. It was sobering realizing that it would be the last night spent in the comfort their homes.

* * * * * * * * * * * * * * * * * * * *

When the customary bells sounded the following day, the Neu Pasuans ate their breakfast. But the farmers didn't head to the fields, and the children didn't go to school. With a sense of urgency the villagers finished their last-minute packing before hitching up their horses to the wagons. Any livestock left behind would likely starve in their pens, so the gates were flung open to let the animals out to fend for themselves.

Finally everyone was ready. They were ready for the long journey to . . . they didn't know where. Just somewhere away from the structure of village life that was all they had ever known. This was a time of uncertainty, and a thick gloom and unsettling fear surrounded the rows of horses and wagons. October 6, 1944 would be forever etched in their memories.

Before the wagon train was ready to leave, Major Erwin Menge came running up to Tate. "You and your family can travel with us. Our convoy will take along as many citizens as we can handle," he explained. "You may use the camper." The major had grown close with the Wittmann family over the past 11 months.

Mame was pleased at the invitation of joining the German army convoy. She gave a sigh of relief as she cuddled four-month-old baby Herta. The army usually had a food supply with them, and hopefully enough milk for the baby to drink. Without any delay, Tate hitched the camper to the back of one of the big army trucks and began transferring their belongings from the wagon to the camper.

At precisely 1:00 p.m., the whips cracked, the horses followed their masters' commands, and the wagon wheels turned in unison. The Wittmann family stayed behind, tearfully watching as the countless wagons pulled by horse teams headed out of Neu Pasua. Dogs and cats that were left behind sensed trouble, and they began to bark and shriek. Cows and pigs wandered aimlessly about. An eerie loneliness settled over the village.

* * * * * * * * * * * * * * * * * * *

"Friedrich, since we aren't going to leave until evening, is there enough time to butcher a pig?" Mame suggested.

125

Mame's idea was not only a practical one, but it gave them a focused task amidst the upheaval around them.

Typically a pig was boiled until the hair could be scraped off, but there wasn't time for that today. "We'll just burn off the hair," Tate decided as he quickly butchered the pig and rolled it over some burning straw. Then they cut up the meat and packed it into a container.

Mame prepared a full supper, and the Wittmann family sat down to their last meal in their Neu Pasua home. After they had finished eating, Margaretha instinctively began to clear off the table but Tate stopped her. "Why bother doing the dishes for those who will invade and rob us of our home?" he said.

* * * * * * * * * * * * * * * * * *

By 8:00 p.m., the German army was preparing to leave. Aunt Elisabeth (Wilhelm) and Cousin Willie were also among the small group of Neu Pasuan villagers who stayed behind to travel with the army. An army officer invited them to ride in his Volkswagon.

Tate was the last one of Margaretha's family members to get inside the camper. Major Menge came and stood beside him. He must have sensed that Tate was struggling with leaving behind his home and land. The major expressed that he felt badly for them. "What you and your people have done to make the soil so fertile around here cannot be compared to anywhere else . . . . and it's so calm and peaceful here," he pointed out.

When the army convoy reached the outskirts of Neu Pasua, Mame called out anxiously. She had spotted a woman with her two young children standing near a ditch, "Oh, Friedrich! Couldn't they fit in here too? Please, Friedrich."

It was possible that the woman and her children had missed the wagon train. Tate motioned for the army truck to stop, and he helped bring the appreciative little family inside the camper. The convoy continued on, heading northwest. Occasionally the army division would stop for short periods of time to eat, refuel, and service their vehicles.

Even though the camper was crowded with people and belongings, it provided a fairly comfortable means of traveling. But it wasn't really the physical conditions that bothered the Wittmanns . . . it was the distressing, uncertain outlook of their refugee status, and the heartache and disappointment of leaving behind everything that they had ever known.

Family Photo of Uncle Johann and Aunt Margaretha Wittmann-Falkenburger and family taken just prior to passing through Neu Pasua on fleeing day

The Town Crier ～ would beat the drum, then cry out, Hear ye, Hear Ye!

Photo of Neu Pasua's trommler (Hudjetz-Loeber)

* * * * * * * * * * * * * * * * * *

EDITOR NOTE: Margaretha's Deschner and Wittmann grandparents had all passed away prior to fleeing day. On fleeing day, all of the remaining Deschner relatives and the Jakob and Johann Wittmann families left on the wagon train with the majority of the villagers.

Uncle Willhelm was not with his wife and young son because he was away serving as an interpreter for the German army. (Grandfather Wittmann had sent Willhelm to a Serbian school in Vojka to get education beyond the 5th grade. It was there that he had learned the Serbian language.)

Aunt Margaretha and Uncle Johann Falkenburger had already passed through Neu Pasua and were on their way to Austria. Aunt Florina Wittmann and Aunt Elisabeth and Uncle Andreas Betsch and their family still lived in Beška. Because their village was of mixed descent, they didn't receive the same Russian threat like Neu Pasua and some of the other all-German villages.

* * * * * * * * * * * * * * * * * *

EDITOR NOTE: The Yugoslavian cities of Belgrade and Dubrovnik became liberated on October 20, 1944. Yugoslavian and Russian soldiers were released from their imprisonment.

(http://timelines.ws/countries/YUGOSLAVIA.HTML)

10

Austria
Fall 1944

The Friedrich Wittmann family and the other Neu Pasuans traveling with them were able to accompany the German army division until they reached Baranja County, located near the Hungarian border. Left to fend for themselves, the refugee group found shelter with a German-speaking family. They earned their keep by picking grapes in the family's vineyard.

It was during this time that Margaretha's family was surprised and overjoyed to see Wilhelm Wittmann. "Why, Wilhelm!" Mame joyfully greeted her brother-in-law. "How did you find us here?" Margaretha was just as surprised to see her uncle. His wife Aunt Elisabeth and Cousin Willie were among their group of refugees.

"I had a short leave from the army," Uncle Wilhelm explained. "And of course I was anxious to get home. I immediately headed home by train. It was dark when I got to the Neu Pasua train station, and there was only one other man there. It was very late in the evening so I didn't expect to be meeting a lot of people. But this man, whom I didn't even recognize, stumbled towards me and exclaimed, 'Wilhelm Wittmann, what are you doing here? All your people are gone. Don't you know that?' I smelled alcohol on his breath and dismissed his crazy chatter. I didn't believe him, but I began to sense that something was terribly wrong as I got closer to home. My house was abandoned. I went on to your farm; one of your horses was out of the pasture and running wild. Then I spotted some soldiers from the German army. They were slaughtering pigs. They were certainly not lacking food; evidently there was an abundant supply. All of our people had completely vanished! Then I realized that the drunkard had spoken the truth."

Uncle Wilhelm stayed with them for a few days. When he left, he took Aunt Elisabeth and Willie with him. His plan was for the three of them to take the train to Austria so they could meet up with his mother-in-law and other family members who had already fled there. When he was assured that his family was safely reconnected with relatives, he would report back to the German army.

This was also the time when Mame took the opportunity to cook the meat from the pig that they had butchered in Neu Pasua. After cooking the meat, Mame re-packed it within the fat. The pork could be stored in the fat for quite some time before it would spoil.

* * * * * * * * * * * * * * * * * * * *

The German family agreed to drive the company of refugees across the border to the city of Pećs, Hungary. In Pećs, they spotted the division of the German army that they had just parted ways with. Tata begged the soldiers to let the group stay with them. They were permitted to stay in a horse barn close to the army camp. Each morning Tate walked over to the army camp to get their food rations. Daily life consisted of keeping everyone fed, trying to stay as clean as conditions permitted, and waiting and wondering what would happen next.

"Magdalena!" Margaretha heard Tate's stricken voice one morning as he returned from his daily hike to the army camp. "The army is gone!" Again the small company of refugees found themselves alone, and without any food. None of them even knew a word of Hungarian.

Tate and Mame discussed their options. One of the refugee women interrupted their conversation, "You aren't going to leave us here by ourselves, are you?" Tate empathized with all of the fearful women, children, and old men. He took charge of the refugee company and decided to rent three train cars to take them all to Germany. As the refugees lugged their belongings onto the train cars, they only hoped that the train would take them to a safe place where they could be reunited with loved ones as quickly as possible.

When the train passed through Czechoslovakia, Margaretha marveled at the hilly and scenic landscape, which was so different from the flat lands of Neu Pasua. Mame and Tate were preoccupied with their worries about what they might encounter in Germany. The whole family was anxious to be with the familiar faces of their Neu Pasuan relatives and friends.

Baby Herta's fussing soon turned into screaming despite Mame's rocking and soothing. "She needs milk!" Mame despairingly said to Tate. When the train made a stop at the next station, Tate took the opportunity to exit. He hoped to find a local villager who would sell him some milk.

* * * * * * * * * * * * * * * * * *

All too soon the train began to lurch away from the station. Mame shouted helplessly, "Ach, the train is leaving and Tate is not here!" Fritz, Margaretha, and Jakob desperately searched for any signs of Tate.

Miraculously, a breathless Tate appeared in their train car. How thankful the family was to see him. What a scare . . . and, what a delight to see Herta as she ravenously drank the warm milk!

Tate was still catching his breath as he described to Margaretha, Fritz, and Jakob about how panic-stricken he had been. On his way back to the train station with milk in hand, he saw in the distance that the train was already beginning to move away from the station. Tate was sure that he'd never run so fast in his entire life. Somehow he had managed to catch hold of a bar from the last train car to hoist himself up onto the train.

The train continued before stopping again at the first city within the Schlesien region. Tate located a Red Cross office and inquired about where other Neu Pasuan refugees had gone. He learned that many Neu Pasuans had headed to Austria because they were accepting refugees. "We'll take the train and go to Austria too," Tate decided.

The Wittmann family stayed on the train that was headed for St. George, Austria. Someone had informed Tate that Uncle Johann had travelled there. The other refugees from their company got off the train at various stops. But when the train reached St. George, it didn't take them long to realize that the town was already flooded with refugees. And no one wanted to keep a family with six children.

* * * * * * * * * * * * * * * * * * *

EDITOR NOTE: The Schlesien region is now part of Poland. The Russian army invaded that area only two weeks after Margaretha's train travelled through there.

11

Living with the Schirlings
Fall 1944 – Spring 1945

The Schirling family agreed to provide temporary housing for the Wittmann family. They were the fourth refugee family that they had taken in. Mr. Schirling was the mayor of St. George.

The Schirling farm was located in a forested area. A winding stream went through their property. Two of the refugee families lived in a small feed mill near the stream. The Wittmanns were allotted the upper level of the Schirling family's large pig barn. The two rooms had previously been renovated to provide living quarters for their hired help. The other family lived in the homestead with the Schirlings. All of the refugees registered with the Red Cross, something that they were required to do once they found their temporary housing.

At this point in time, the German army was enforcing a military draft. No man was overlooked, regardless of age or disability. If any man refused to join the German army or bear arms, they were immediately thrown into prison. Tate initially had reservations about leaving the family, but dutifully enlisted.

It was a difficult time for the refugee women, and they all shared a common heartache. While their husbands and older sons were away from home, they had to singlehandedly raise their young children and make provisions for daily food. Mame learned that Katarina Schumacher, a widow from Neu Pasua, was living in a very undesirable situation. At her request, the Schirlings permitted Katarina and her son Michael to move in with their family.

The Wittmann family made every attempt to be helpful, and not a hindrance, to the Schirlings. Jakob and Florina went to school, and Fritz kept busy chopping firewood for Mr. Schirling. Margaretha's daily job was to milk four of the Schirling family's cows. Altogether there were about 20 cows on their farm. The Schirling family's two milk maids were both widows who had several younger children. By milking two cows for each milk maid, Margaretha helped ease their workload.

Because the war had caused such a shortage of food and supplies, the Austrian government provided their citizens and refugees with ration cards. The ration cards allowed only a limited amount of the rationed items. Even though the Wittmann family had six children, they were allotted only one loaf of bread per day. The loaf of bread was so small that Tate could have eaten it all by himself! But they were thankful for whatever they could get to eat.

* * * * * * * * * * * * * * * * *

"Gretle, I need you to watch Magdalena and baby Herta," Mame instructed Margaretha one morning after breakfast. "I have to walk to town and pick up our supplies." Margaretha was delighted with the opportunity of being in charge of the household.

Magdalena and Herta played well together. Four-year-old Magdalena had beautiful big brown eyes, and Mama always styled her dark hair into two thick braids. Herta, now about a year old, resembled her older sister Florina with her blonde hair and gorgeous blue eyes.

With her ration cards in hand, Mame headed out the door. Margaretha spent the next couple of hours working diligently. She tidied up the rooms and swept and scrubbed the floors. She was interrupted by the sound of the girls' laughter.

From the second-story window, Margaretha could see Jakob running alongside the Schirling's ram. Jakob quickly darted in front of the ram as he playfully handled his curly horns. The ram reacted to the teasing by giving Jakob a strong buck. Jakob skillfully escaped to the ram's side and resumed the teasing by tickling it. Around and around they went, keeping Florina and the little girls amused until he finally lost interest with the irritated ram. Margaretha smiled as she returned to her housework. These were carefree days for them on the Schirling farm.

"Sparkling clean!" explained Mame upon her return from town. Margaretha beamed with pride as Mama glanced approvingly around the room. "The air was so fresh on my walk into town," Mame continued. "The mountains are good for the lungs . . . the healthiest I've felt in a long time."

Although Mame didn't complain, Margaretha knew that her health was poor. Even back in Neu Pasua, her anemic condition often affected her. During the summer months, Tate would send Mame to a cottage in the mountainous region near Novi Sad, Yugoslavia to give her a "change of air." Margaretha had many fond memories of joining Mame during her summer vacation. They'd go to restaurants for treats, and take walks through the hilly and scenic region. Tate and Fritz would join them on the weekends. It was in Novi Sad where Tate had bought Margaretha her first wristwatch.

"Now, Gretle," Mame interrupted her daydreaming, "You'd better get your cows milked." Margaretha obediently headed towards the pasture. On her way, she saw Mrs. Schirling standing in front of the house with a rosary as she routinely did every Saturday before supper. The two milk maids were already rounding up the cows. They pranced around the pasture as they sang their Catholic prayers.

There was always a plentiful supply of creamy, delicious milk. Margaretha loved drinking it. Once, when Tate came home for a brief visit, the children filled up on the pudding that Mame made with the milk so that Tate could eat their one loaf of bread.

* * * * * * * * * * * * * * * * * * *

Margaretha missed Tate and she thought about him often. She wondered how long it would be before the war would finally end so that they could all be together again. According to Tate's letters, he was stationed in Braunau, Austria. His letters expressed how he missed the family and could hardly wait until he could see them again. Tate also wrote about how he and the other soldiers craved cigarettes.

Margaretha begged Mame to let her go to Braunau to deliver a care package to Tate. Mame wouldn't consent—it was just too unsafe for a girl to travel by herself. But when her cousin, Adam Maier, agreed to go with Margaretha, Mame said she could go.

The two of them took a train to Braunau. Soldiers, all dressed alike, were everywhere. It was a miracle when they finally found Tate among them. Tate was excited to see them, and he showed Margaretha and Adam his living quarters—an underground bunker. He was very appreciative of the care package that they had brought for him. Late in the evening, Margaretha and Adam took the train back to St.George.

* * * * * * * * * * * * * * * * * * *

War stories were a common theme in adult conversations. Airplanes with roaring engines soaring through the sky were also daily reminders of war. One day, while Margaretha and some other children were playing outside, they spotted a man coming down from the sky in a parachute. He landed in the middle of a field. Filled with curiosity, the children ran to the scene.

"Who are you? What happened? Where are you from?" Margaretha and the children bombarded the parachuter with questions at the same time. The man did not speak German, and his face only reflected fear and pain. He quickly gathered his things together and hurried away. Perhaps his plane had been shot down.

Another time, a jeep pulled into the Schirling farm yard. Men from the American army had come to check up on things. Not only were these men American soldiers, but they happened to be of African descent. Margaretha was terrified—she had never before encountered a colored person in her very sheltered life back in Neu Pasua.

As the soldiers walked towards the barn, Margaretha noticed large white teeth opening and closing between dark lips. She froze in fear. What were these strange men doing with their mouths opening and closing?

Margaretha soon discovered that the soldiers were simply chewing gum. She had never even heard about such a thing as chewing gum. Much to the childrens' delight, the soldiers gave them some as a treat!

* * * * * * * * * * * * * * * * * *

In the spring of 1945, a haggard-looking Tate ambled up the driveway of the Schirling farm. Margaretha was thrilled to see him and eager to hear about his army experiences. He shared how the Americans had invaded Austria and had overtaken the German army division he had been drafted into. They ended up in a prisoner of war camp where they were given only three potatoes a day.

The war conditions, along with the potato diet, left him in a much-weakened state. After two weeks in the POW camp, the Americans released the German soldiers. Finally the family was together again! Adam, another one of Katarina Schumacher's sons who had been serving in the German army, was also released from the army and came to live with them.

* * * * * * * * * * * * * * * * * *

EDITOR NOTE: It was later rumored that, true to the trommler's warning, the Russian army did come to Neu Pasua. The very small group of Neu Pasuans who did not flee with the rest of the village were rounded up and forced into a building. An inspector selected the older and sickly-appearing ones and marched them back out of the building. Gunshots were heard by the people still inside. The fate of the others was not much better. They were sent off to a concentration camp.

* * * * * * * * * * * * * * * * * * *

EDITOR NOTE: On March 7, 1945, the Communist government of Yugoslavia under Tito was formed.
                          (http://timelines.ws/countries/YUGOSLAVIA.HTML)

12

End of the War
June – July 1945

As summer drew near, the hay on the Schirling farm grew bountifully. All of the refugees living there diligently helped with cutting, raking, and turning the hay. After the hay dried in the warm sunshine, it was piled high on the wagons with pitchforks.

The Wittmanns were grateful to the benevolent Shirling family for their kindness. They had been living in Austria for about six months before the long-awaited news finally reached their farm: **"The war is now over. You are free to go back to your homeland!"**

Everyone—from the refugees to the Austrians—was overjoyed to hear the good news. "Finally we can go back home," Tate said.

"Ach, Friedrich, I'd rather not," Mame said apprehensively. "I just don't have a good feeling about going back."

"I'll discuss it with Johann," Tate replied, and headed directly to the farm where his brother was staying.

Upon his return, Mame was anxious to hear what had been decided. "We just settled on each family doing as they see fit," Tate announced. "But we'll all definitely go to Camp Ried. That's where many of the Neu Pasuan refugees are staying. Then, we'll see from there."

Mame was willing to support whatever Tate thought was best, so she began the process of packing up their belongings. But Margaretha could tell that Mame was still troubled, and that her heart was not really into her task. "Why not go home?"

Tate tried to reason with Mame. "We are refugees here in Austria. In Yugoslavia, we have a nice home and farm to go back to. The war is over."

"I don't want to go home either," fifteen-year-old Fritz emphatically stated. "It's so nice here. Why can't we stay? I sure don't want to end up getting slaughtered by some Communist."

Tate laughed. "Ach, Fritz, we didn't hurt anyone. In Neu Pasua, we were citizens of good standing, and we have always lived in peace among our Serbian neighbors. Aren't you anxious to get back to our farm?"

Mr. Schirling agreed to take all five of his refugee families by wagon to Camp Ried. At Camp Ried, families registered their names and hometowns. Refugees grouped together and excitedly exchanged their plans for the future. Everyone was eager to get home and to get on with their lives.

Margaretha overheard a man from Neu Pasua as he spoke to Tate and Uncle Johann about his fear and uncertainty of going back home. "Now he's got reason to be concerned," Tate commented to Uncle Johann after the man walked away. "Don't you remember how he used to parade around in his tall army boots as he tried to stop the Serbs from passing through Neu Pasua?"

Tate was interrupted when an official at the train station began reading off a long list of refugee names. The refugees were on edge about who would be the privileged ones to board the first train back home to Yugoslavia. Priority, of course, was given to the Serbian POWs. Any remaining space would be filled with refugees. How excited Margaretha was when she heard three of the Wittmann families' names announced: Jakob, Friedrich, and Johann. Now they could all return to their beautiful life in Neu Pasua!

They waited all day before a train finally arrived at the station. The Serbian POWs boarded the train, followed by several hundred refugees which included almost 200 residents from Neu Pasua. The other refugees were from surrounding Yugoslavian villages. A majority of the refugees were women and children because many of the men were still POWs. Tate, of course, had been released from his POW camp by the American soldiers. The whole Friedrich Wittmann family was together: Tate, Mame, Fritz, Margaretha, Jakob, Florina, Magdalena, and Herta.

Uncle Jakob and Aunt Elisabeth got on the train with their children Jakob, Margaretha, and Elisabeth. Uncle Jakob had been exempt from the draft because he was over fifty years old. Uncle Johann and Aunt Elisabeth with their children Florina, Liese, Katrina, Johann, and Barbara also boarded the train. Uncle Johann couldn't serve in the army because of the issues he had from a gastric surgery.

The Wittmann families grouped together in the same train car. The seats had all been removed, and everyone tried to get comfortable by sitting on their luggage. There were windows to look out of, and there was a sliding door on one side of their train car. Finally they were heading back to their homes in Neu Pasua! The refugees who had not been able to get on the first train expressed their extreme disappointment. One woman sobbed uncontrollably as the train pulled away from the station.

* * * * * * * * * * * * * * * * * * *

It was a hot summer day on July 6, 1945, and Margaretha was excited. Tomorrow would be her fourteenth birthday! Their train car's sliding door was left partly open to let in the gentle breeze. Margaretha, Liese, and some of the other cousins dangled their feet over the edge of their train car while they cheerily sang *"In Der Heimat."*

It seemed, though, that no matter which region the train passed through, the landscape and buildings looked dismal from the debris and ruin caused by the bombings. Somewhere in the province of Slovenia, the train made a stop. American soldiers handed out bread. The bread didn't have any color or flavor. It was very different from the rye and dark grain breads that Margaretha was accustomed to. She could hardy chew the soft bread because it kept sticking to the roof of her mouth and getting wedged between her teeth.

The train crossed freely through the Croatia-Yugoslavia border. No one was required to show any identification. The train continued past the city of Maribor.

* * * * * * * * * * * * * * * * * * *

The train made an unexpected stop, and several armed men entered their train car. Everyone was taken by surprise when the intruders began demanding items such as watches, jewelry, and radios. And then they disappeared. What was this all about?

Uneasiness settled upon the passengers, and there was an eerie silence as the train continued for hours along the railway. Then the train slowed down as it switched onto another railway track. "We're not on the right track!" Tate spoke up in alarm. "This is only a single railway. The rail line home is a double track since it's a main railway!" Margaretha sensed a heightened alertness and fear among the refugee train passengers. Where was the train taking them?

Tate guessed that the train was headed in the direction of Zagreb, the capitol city of Croatia. It continued along the track for a little while longer before making another sudden stop. Margaretha wondered why the train had stopped there. It wasn't even at a train station. Then more armed guards abruptly stormed into their train car. All of the passengers were ordered to exit the train. Their awful fear became a reality— they were being hijacked!

Everyone was forced to carry all their heavy suitcases. It was not easy to tell how far they were made to walk before they got to a very large shed-like building with a rounded roof. They were commanded to put all of their belongings inside the building. Several Serbian messages were announced over a loud speaker. "What are they saying?" Mame asked Tate.

"Something like 'Germans, don't play with your lives,'" Tate responded. Thankfully Tate had learned a little Serbian back in Neu Pasua.

Armed guards surrounded them from all sides, and they began separating the men from the women. For no apparent reason, all of the refugees were being treated very harshly. No one understood why. The men were taken into one of the rooms while the women and children were left standing in the main entranceway of the building.

A few men, including Tate, managed to escape from a window and seek out their families. "Put on as many clothes as possible," Tate whispered to Margaretha and the rest of her trembling family. "You won't be able to take anything else with you." Fritz managed to hide a ham underneath his coat.

Later, on that same evening, some of the guards made a small opening with the sliding door. One by one they ordered Margaretha and the other captives through the opening. It was in this manner that they took every remaining piece of jewelry and every other important object that they had with them.

If the women didn't remove their earrings quickly enough, they were torn from their ears by the guards. Margaretha hurriedly removed her golden earrings, the ones she had once longed for, and threw them into the suitcase set by the doorway. As Mame walked through the doorway clutching one-year-old baby Herta, one of the guards snatched the little blanket that Mame had wrapped tightly around her. Apparently these hard-hearted guards felt that even a baby captive deserved no warmth or comfort.

Some of the guards had thrown many of the refugees' belongings into a large pile before setting it on fire. Sadly it included Mama's Bible, hymnal, and the family photo album that she had so carefully worked on back in Neu Pasua.

* * * * * * * * * * * * * * * * * * *

EDITOR NOTE: Unfortunately the three Wittmann families happened to be on one of the first trains that made its way back to Yugoslavia after the war had been declared over. One of the German refugee train passengers escaped after they were initially raided by the armed men. He made his way back to Camp Ried to alert the other refugees about the train hijacking incident. No more refugees from Camp Ried boarded the trains headed for Yugoslavia. The other Neu Pasuan refugees—including the Deschner relatives—remained in Austria to continue working for the farmers. Eventually, most of them immigrated to Germany.

* * * * * * * * * * * * * * * * * * *

EDITOR NOTE: Margaretha stated that the Yugoslavians wanted to deport the German-speaking refugees back to Austria. However, Austria was already overrun by refugees and didn't want them either.

13

The Long Walk
July 1945

Margaretha and all of the other captives were forced to board another train. It was a cattle train—roofless with sides about four feet high. Everyone was pressed so tightly against each other that they were essentially forced to stand. A heavy rain poured relentlessly down on them from the night sky.

It was difficult to know just how far they traveled. When they were finally let out of the train, everyone was rounded up like cattle by the armed guards who surrounded them. All night long they were forced to walk. The leader found that his fist was an effective way to speak, and a punch in the chest was common for the men.

Into the next day they continued to walk. All day long they were made to walk, walk, and then walk some more. Tate carried Magdalena because her little legs just couldn't endure the neverending walk. Herta clung onto Fritz's shoulders as he carried her on his back, and Mame walked wearily beside them. Margaretha, Jakob, and Florina made sure that they stayed close to the family. No one wanted to get separated.

The soldiers didn't bother feeding them. Whenever they passed through a village, Margaretha and the other desperate captives begged for food. It was at the center of the village when Mame would take baby Herta in her arms as she cried out to the villagers. They seemed to have more sympathy when they saw little ones, and food was often tossed in her direction.

Unfortunately, the majority of Neu Pasuan captives could only speak German, and the villagers in this area spoke only Serbian. Whenever Margaretha received a good portion of food, she shared some with Tate, who just couldn't succumb to begging.

Day and night the people walked.   When it got dark, and only when it was permissible, the exhausted captives stumbled to the side of the road to sleep.   But when daylight came, they were rudely awakened and forced to continue in their long and dreary march to an unknown destination.

* * * * * * * * * * * * * * * * * *

After numerous days of walking, the conditions began taking their toll, especially on the frail and elderly.   Uncle Jakob's mother-in-law, Margaretha, became weaker and weaker.   She had been eager to leave Austria to get back to Neu Pasua and be reunited with her husband, Friedrich.   On fleeing day, Friedrich was suffering from a hernia and chose to stay behind.   He had claimed that he couldn't possibly endure the long hours of sitting on the wagon.

Now old Margaretha could no longer go on.   Since those who lagged behind were beaten, Uncle Johann and Tate clasped their hands together and carried her between them.   Soon a local farmer passed by with his horse and wagon.   Several of the weak and elderly captives begged for a ride.   Old Margaretha took off one of her skirts and gave it to the farmer as payment.   For some reason, the guards allowed it—they probably didn't know what else to do with them.

Eventually the captives were led through the village of Varaždin.   It was very late in the evening when they arrived at an old factory that had been used to make culverts.   They were left with no options but to spend the night sleeping on the floor inside the factory.

The next day everyone was forced outside to a small confined area.   As the day went on, the sun got hotter and hotter.   It left the hundreds of hungry refugees feeling crowded and weak.

Several cement culverts lay strewn about. Jakob and Florina crawled into one, hoping to get some relief from the hot sun; however, it wasn't long before they crawled back out. It was just as hot inside the culverts!

A kettle of bean soup was made on the premises. When it was ready, the hungry captives quickly formed a line. What a disappointment to find it was tasteless, and made without salt or seasonings.

* * * * * * * * * * * * * * * * * *

After several days of this tasteless soup, Margaretha was determined to get something to help flavor the soup. Looking for just the right moment when the armed guards weren't glancing in her direction, she managed to escape from their confined area.

Margaretha knocked on the door of one of the Varaždin village homes. The Serbian woman who answered the door had a surprised look on her face when she saw Margaretha standing there. What a sight she must have been with her tangled hair and wrinkled dress from being worn days on end! She tried to explain her request for salt as best as she could. But the woman only shook her head sadly as she displayed her empty cupboards. The villagers must not have had any salt either.

The people tried to comfort and encourage one another, seeking out those they recognized within their midst. But the days only seemed to get longer with no place to go, nothing to do, and a mountain of uncertainty before them. Would they ever get back home? Would they forever be captives? What did the Yugoslavian government have against them?

Although physically strained from their circumstances, little Herta still managed to be somewhat energetic. Her blond hair, blue eyes, and sweet smile won many hearts. It was on one of those long and hot days that Herta took her first steps. She toddled from one sibling to the other. After numerous

148

shaky steps and falls, she became a little steadier on her feet. Soon she was walking with a grin of satisfaction. What a sliver of joy in the midst of their bleak circumstances!

While they were at Varaždin, Uncle Jakob's mother-in-law Margaretha died. Uncle Jakob approached one of the soldiers for permission to bury her in a local graveyard. The guard consented, since he didn't have any plans to bury her himself.

14

Velika Pisanica and Krndia
July – October 1945

S oon, under the ever watchful eyes of the armed guards, the captives were again forced to walk. This time they were led to Velika Pisanica, where they were confined in an abandoned soccer field. Tate immediately surveyed their boundaries, and the many guards that moved constantly about them. He came to the conclusion that it was impossible for a family of eight to escape.

Everyone slept on the ground. And when it rained, they got soaked. There were no dry clothes to put on because all they had were the clothes on their backs. Most of the summer days were sunny, and there was nothing to shield them from the hot sun that beat unmercifully down on them day after day.

The meals usually consisted of beans or a soup made with overripe peas that were cooked in a large kettle. Except for the liquid in their meager servings of soup, there was no drinking water available. At times the pea soup had a lot of bugs floating in it, and Margaretha would shudder at the repulsive meal. "Ach, Gretle, just close your eyes and eat," Tate would say despairingly. He knew that they needed every ounce of nourishment possible.

* * * * * * * * * * * * * * * * * *

One day, Uncle Andreas Betsch appeared in their midst. They had no idea how he had gotten there, but word must have spread to him that his three brothers-in-law and their families had been captured and taken to Velika Pisanica. Miraculosly he even managed to sneak in some food and money. Uncle

Andreas took a huge risk by entering the camp, but his fluency in Serbian must have been to his advantage.

Uncle Andreas was appalled at their living conditions. "You're living even worse than the gypsies," Margaretha heard him say to Tate. Before he left, Uncle Andreas reassured his relatives that he would be praying for their release from captivity so they could all return to their homes in Neu Pasua.

* * * * * * * * * * * * * * * * * *

Besides the Neu Pasuans, there were several others within the camp that Margaretha's parents recognized. Heinrich Miller was a church elder from the Crwinka Nazarean Church. Margaretha often witnessed Mame and Tate having intent conversations with him. Heinrich Miller provided the much-needed spiritual and emotional support, and he helped to renew their faith and courage in the Lord. Even in their bleak and uncertain circumstance, the forlorn captives found comfort in a funeral service that Heinrich Miller held for a Neu Pasuan man who had died there.

Life continued under the cruel treatment of the Serbian guards. Later in the fall, when the weather became bitterly cold, Margaretha and the other captives were permitted to go into the animal stalls of some nearby barns. But aside from this small comfort, there seemed to be no end to their misery.

* * * * * * * * * * * * * * * * * *

One day the guards began picking out the strongest young men and women and separating them from the rest of the group. When a guard pointed his gun at Fritz, Margaretha witnessed the most distressing sight she had ever seen. Tate broke down, tears streaming uncontrollably down the sides of his cheeks as his family was separated. The guards also pointed their guns at two of Margaretha's cousins; Uncle Jakob's seventeen-year-old son Jakob, and Uncle Johann's seventeen-year-old daughter Florina. The group was quickly herded away to what would most likely be the Russian forced-labor camps. These were rumored to have the worst living conditions imaginable. Margaretha wondered if they'd ever see Fritz and her cousins again.

The rest of the captives were forced to begin walking. With armed guards positioned all around the group, they continued their dreary march through the countryside and past other small villages until they got to Krndia. A district of Krndia that had been occupied by German Yugoslavians prior to the war had now been turned into a concentration camp. All three Wittmann families were allotted only a small room of a house.

Living conditions in Krndia were not much better than in Velika Pisanica. At night, when they began to lay themselves down on the floor to sleep, there wasn't nearly enough space. "We'll take turns," Tate suggested. The others agreed. Half of the adults and older children went outside so that the others could sleep. Then, later in the night, they switched places.

Even in the awful living conditions, the natural events of life happened. A woman who lived in the Wittmann's neighborhood back in Neu Pasua gave birth to a baby boy.

* * * * * * * * * * * * * * * * * *

Margaretha enjoyed going to Heinrich Miller's area of the camp. His daughter, Maria, taught her and Cousin Liese how to sing many hymns. "Blessed Zion, Be Contented" soon became one of their favorite hymns because many of the stanzas fit so perfectly with their present situation.

As the girls sang, the words gave them comfort and provided a diversion from their miserable conditions. *"If with anguish thou art shaken, If men bind and torture thee, Thou wilt never be forsaken—Think upon eternity! Stand in faith and do not fear, For thy Lord is ever near. Zion, let His hand direct thee; He will strengthen and protect thee!"* (Apostolic Christian Hymnal)

Mame spent many hours praying for Fritz and the other young men and women who were so cruelly torn away from their families. They had no way of keeping in touch. And they had no way of knowing if they were dead or alive.

* * * * * * * * * * * * * * * * * *

Some time passed before Margaretha and the group of captives were rounded up yet again. Fortunately the walk to the next destination was not as long. How thrilled they were to find that they were headed to a train station! Instructions were given to get into groups according to home provinces. The Neu Pasuans grouped together with others from the province of Srem.

The Yugoslavian government must have realized that the captives' only desire was to return to their peaceable farm lives. None of them had caused any trouble. Surely they had endured enough suffering. Hopes soared as they were finally allowed to board another train.

At the village of Vinkovci, the train made a stop. People from that province, including Heinrich Miller and his family, stepped off the train. Uncle Jakob leaned over to Margaretha and her cousins. "Now, when we smell the air of our own province Srem, that will mean we're almost home," he said with relief in his voice.

SECTION THREE:

Concentration Camp

15

Initiation to the Swilara
November 1945

T he train that held the captives traveled to Sremska, Mitrovica before coming to an abrupt halt. Instantly, Margaretha saw even more armed guards surrounding their train. Then all of the people were forced to get out. The guards waved their guns as they angrily yelled out commands in Serbian. What was this all about?

Delusional and fearful, the captives had no choice but to obey. Lined on all sides by the armed guards, the large group of captives was marched into the city of Mitrovica. Eventually they were led into a yard outside of a two-story silk factory made of old brick. Tall, barbed wire fences encircled them.

A young man, cold and merciless, seemed to be in charge. His eyes were wild with hatred as he screamed obscenities at them. Terrified, Margaretha drew close to her family, alongside all of the other misfortunate German-speaking captives. If they didn't respond to their orders quickly enough, the guards would stomp on their toes or jab them with rifles.

All around Margaretha children cried, women wept, and the few men in their midst tried to console their families. But any emotional expressions of fear or sympathy among the captives only seemed to intensify the young man's fury, resulting in even more severe punishment. The men were frequently punched in the stomach.

It was difficult for Margaretha to hide her frantic emotions as she stood in the line formation that was ordered by the guards. Margaretha observed some people wandering aimlessly about from behind another fenced-in area. They had such funny-looking heads and appeared very thin and sickly. She shivered and looked away.

One by one each individual from their group was stripped and searched. When Uncle Jakob was interrogated, the guards discovered that he had some German money in his possession. They grabbed the bills and furiously threw them on the ground. Then they roughly tied his hands behind his back and left him standing there, naked and humiliated. At the earliest opportunity, Tate tossed his coat over Uncle Jakob's shoulders.

During the search, they were commanded to open their mouths. Any teeth that contained gold fillings were knocked out by the end of a rifle. Then they were made to stand in another line.

Margaretha watched the people in line ahead of her. One after the other, they were roughly shoved into a chair, and their hair was completely shaved off. Now she realized why those prisoners' heads had looked so strange. Tears welled up in her eyes. She glanced back at Mame, and in the next instant Margaretha's large, thick braids were on the ground. How naked and ashamed she felt! Then Mame's beautiful head of hair was shaved off too. It was a strange and awkward sight.

Not long afterwards, Margaretha's stomach churned from the bitter smell that filled the air as the huge pile of hair was burned. Now, stripped of all dignity, the hundreds of captives were left with absolutely nothing but the clothes on their backs.

* * * * * * * * * * * * * * * * * *

The large group of captives was taken inside the old run-down silk factory, called "Swilara" in Serbian. They were led up a long set of stairs to the second floor. The air was filled with the rancid stench of urine and feces.

Men, seemingly hundreds of them, were sitting or lying about. There was no furniture. There was nothing but men on the floor surrounded by four bare walls. They appeared thin, haggard, and worn. Some of the men glanced up at Margaretha's group as they walked through their living quarters, but many of them did not pay them much heed.

Margaretha watched as an older man limped to a large kettle standing in the center of the room. Realizing that the kettle served as their toilet, Margaretha quickly turned her head. There just wasn't any privacy.

Then the group was led up another set of stairs. Margaretha gasped involuntarily as they entered the dark attic. She wanted to shut out the repulsive scene that lay before her. Not only was there the rancid smell of urine and feces, but also the overwhelming odor of decaying bodies.

As Margaretha's eyes began to adjust to her dim surroundings, she saw figures slightly moving on wooden boards. Could these figures really be people? In horror, she watched as they held their bald heads with their trembling hands. Their eyes were sunk deep into their faces, and their ears were paper thin. Their ribs protruded, and each bone was visible underneath their translucent skin. They seemed to have no stomach at all. Many were moaning, praying, or breathing shallow breaths of stale air. Some weakly cried out for loved ones who weren't there.

The misery was too intense. Margaretha could hardly bear looking at the grotesque prisoners. And she knew that this wasn't a dream. Shuddering, she wanted to hide herself in Mame's skirt but she knew she needed to be strong for her younger brother and sisters.

In the meantime, Uncle Jakob had been released and sent up to the attic with the rest of the relatives. He shook his bowed head to the group and whispered despondently, "There's absolutely no way that we'll be able to get out of this place alive!" A cold fear settled in Margaretha's stomach. Would they all end up like these miserable figures?

Night came, and as the temperature got colder and colder, the newcomers had no choice but to huddle closely together in their attempt to stay warm. The small amount of straw that lay strewn on the attic floor was all they had to sleep on, and it was way too sparse to keep out the late November chill. Margaretha was hungry, thirsty, cold, and fearful. She found it nearly impossible to sleep. She closed her eyes, and hoped that when she reopened them, the nightmare would be ended.

* * * * * * * * * * * * * * * * * *

Morning brought no relief, and the dreaded truth was foremost in Margaretha's mind—she and her family were prisoners in a place where the inhuman conditions would not be able to sustain life for long. Margaretha glanced at the awful scene still before her. She was sure that some of the prisoners who had moved feebly about just yesterday would now be laying cold and dead.

Margaretha heard a pitiful sobbing from across the attic room. It came from the woman who delivered a baby while in the Krndia camp. The woman's body was trembling as she clung tightly to her cold and lifeless infant. The poor living conditions, lack of nutrition, and the freezing night had been too much.

A shrill bell rang. The new prisoners quickly learned that the young man who was in charge when they first arrived at the Swilara was called the corporal. With his cruel leadership, he made sure that everyone knew it. The prisoners also learned that it was of utmost importance to line up promptly when the bell rang.

As Margaretha hurried to line up, she could not take her eyes off of the frail and pathetic-looking prisoners. Some limped or shuffled along with an awkward gait. Those who were too weak to even stand up were left behind.

The line moved quickly past the food kettle. Margaretha was disappointed to be served only a small piece of dry "cornbread." She choked back her tears and whispered hoarsely to Tate. "I can't eat this."

"It's all we'll get. You have to eat it." Tate tried to encourage her.

Margaretha looked down at her small piece of stale cornbread. It could hardly be considered a meager portion. She was so hungry, and yet she could hardly eat. She felt nauseated, and her nostrils would not be relieved of the relentless stench that could be smelled everywhere.

* * * * * * * * * * * * * * * * * *

EDITOR NOTE: The Swabians were now a people without a country. Concentration camps were established to obliterate the people of German descent. The Swilara at Mitrovica was one of the most dreaded and cruel concentration camps, partly because the heartless young nineteen-year-old corporal in charge. The shock of the first day that Margaretha entered the Mitrovica concentration camp will be forever etched in her memory.

16

More Newcomers
December 1945

A fter several days of living in the attic of the Swilara, the guards separated the men and older boys from the women and children. Margaretha's heart ached when she saw one of the guards roughly shoving Tate towards the group of men. Tate, who once had been so strong and confident, now looked old and frail.

Their worth and dignity were being systematically destroyed! First their train was hijacked, then they were stripped of their personal belongings and left with hardly enough clothes on their backs. In Velika Pisanica, Fritz was torn away from the family. Here at the Swilara their hair was shaved, and they were forced to stay in a dreary attic filled with dying people. Through all of the suffering they'd endured, they had at least been together as a family. But now even that was being taken away from them.

Mame, Margaretha, young Jakob (whom the guards did not force to go with the men), Florina, Magdalena, and Herta were sent to the first floor, the living quarters of hundreds of women. They searched for an empty bed among the make-shift bunks. Margaretha worried about Tate and wondered if they'd ever see Fritz again.

The barbed wire fence surrounding the Swilara was a stark reminder that they were prisoners. After a disappointing trek for stale cornbread, Margaretha still felt hungry. Her bare scalp prickled against the cold and her whole body itched. Even brushing away the straw did not relieve the itching. It didn't take long for them to realize that lice abounded everywhere.

"I can't stand these bugs." Florina began to sob.

Soon the dreadful days began blurring together. Food was usually served only once or twice a day. Often it was only a small chunk of corn mush slightly cooked in water, and ground up with the cobs like cattle feed. Ugly, raw mush. The measly portions were not enough to live on, and just barely enough to avert death. They were not given any water to drink, even though there was a well on the premises. The well was locked and only opened occasionally for cooking.

* * * * * * * * * * * * * * * * * * *

On a freezing cold day, under the direction of the cruel corporal, all of the men and women were sent outside. There they were forced to stand on the cold ice and snow. A fence separated the men and women, and none of them were permitted to speak to each other. All day long they stood for no reason at all, and without any food. Margaretha occasionally peered out the window while she worried about Mame and Tate, and at the same time she tried to comfort her siblings.

On another day, they suffered a cruel trick when the afternoon bell signaling a meal went off. Vile as the food was, their starving stomachs craved whatever they could get. With only about thirty minutes allowed to feed hundreds of people, the prisoners had learned to be efficient. But instead of a kettle of food, there was only some straw that had been scattered on the ground.

The corporal enjoyed watching their hope for a morsel of food being crushed. He screamed at the weak prisoners as he commanded that they pick up every last bit of straw. If they didn't move quickly enough, they were beaten. Margaretha could tell that Uncle Johann was having a hard time bending over as he reached down for the straw. She bit her lip when she witnessed one of the guards roughly shoving him to the ground.

Margaretha turned her face away from him and worked as diligently as she could. "Why?" Margaretha wondered.

What had they done to anger the officials? How did they become prisoners in this horrible, horrible place? There weren't any answers. Only one thing could sustain her— her faith in God. In times like these Margaretha hummed in her mind the songs that Heinrich Miller's daughter had taught her back in the camp at Krndia.

* * * * * * * * * * * * * * * * * *

"Line up!" screeched a guard. It wasn't unusual for the guards to scream at them, but because mealtime had already passed, Margaretha wondered what was going on. But she had learned to obey, because disobedience, or even a slight delay in response to a command, would bring a swift blow from the rifle or an angry stomp on the toes. Mame picked up little Herta, and Margaretha and Florina held onto Magdalena's hands as they stood in line with the other women and children.

Everyone was ordered to encircle a very large freshly dug hole. Beside the hole lay a pile of dead bodies, the ones that had been collected on a daily basis throughout the Swilara. The stiff bodies were naked. Their clothes had been removed by the prisoners themselves because it was a means of survival in their attempts to stay warm.

Several of the prisoners were commanded to throw the bodies into the hole, which turned out to be a massive grave. Because it was freezing cold that day, there wasn't the usual scent of human decay. There was just dead silence, and all that could be heard was the sickening thud of the bodies as they fell one by one into the hole. Each life had been cut short by the abuse and starvation.

As the dead bodies were being thrown into the pit, prisoners would recognize family members or friends. The corporal watched their faces carefully for any show of emotion. And when he found a target, he gleefully administered blows with his swinging rifle. The corporal could not seem to get his fill of torturing his fellow countrymen of German descent.

* * * * * * * * * * * * * * * * * * *

One rainy day, a new group of captives arrived at the Swilara. Margaretha noticed them as she glanced out of the window. They looked cold and miserable as the rain poured steadily down on them. Margaretha felt sorry for them. She had experienced the same mistreatment only a few weeks earlier, and she would give anything to erase the shock, horror, and humiliation from her mind.

Mame had been looking over Margaretha's shoulder. "Gretle . . . that looks like the group that Fritz, Jakob, and Florina were taken away with!" she exclaimed. A glimmer of hope appeared in Mame's pained and weary eyes.

"Look! There he is!" Mame excitedly pointed towards a boy whose eyes were hidden underneath his cap. Margaretha wondered how Mame could ever have recognized him. But it was Fritz! They spotted their cousins Jakob and Florina too.

* * * * * * * * * * * * * * * * * * *

Hours later, Cousin Florina joined them in the women's quarters. It was a bittersweet reunion, and she told them everything that had happened since their separation at Velika Pisanica. She also told them that Fritz and Jakob had been sent upstairs to the men's floor.

Day after day the weary prisoners lived in constant coldness inside the Swilara. The Swilara reeked with the smell of death, and cries of sorrow echoed daily throughout the concentration camp. It didn't take long before they all began to resemble the prisoners who had horrified them upon their arrival. Some prisoners did not even find it worthwhile to line up for food any more. Instead, they hoped that total starvation would hasten their death.

On December 19, Cousin Margaretha relayed the news to Mame that Aunt Elisabeth had died. Later that day, Mame saw Uncle Jakob with his hands and face buried in the fence that separated the men from the women. He also must have heard the awful news about his wife's death. He whispered hoarsely to Mama through the fence, "I'm almost dead too . . . just barely alive." Two days later, on December 21, Uncle Jakob died. His daughter, Elisabeth, also starved to death before the year's end.

* * * * * * * * * * * * * * * * * * *

EDITOR NOTE: Thankfully Fritz and the other two Wittmann cousins did not end up in Russia. Instead, they were taken to a forced labor camp in Gradiste. Somehow, they managed to get word to their single Aunt Florina Wittmann who lived in Beška. They made her aware of their imprisonment in Gradiste.

Aunt Florina traveled alone to Gradiste in search of her niece and nephews. As she neared the prison grounds, she was careful to avoid any suspicious behaviors. As she observed the workers, she noticed a young girl loading bricks onto a wagon. The girl looked like Cousin Florina, yet appeared thinner and more haggard than she had remembered. When Aunt Florina was certain that the young girl was indeed her niece Florina, she slipped up onto the wagon. She tried to appear like she was one of the workers. They talked while they worked, and Aunt Florina handed her a food package. Aunt Florina also managed to find Jakob and Fritz chopping reeds that would later be used for basketmaking. She handed them a food package as well before leaving Gradiste.

* * * * * * * * * * * * * * * * * * *

EDITOR NOTE: *Margaretha stated that she never actually witnessed anyone being shot for trying to escape from the Mitrovica concentration camp, but there were rumors of it. As far as she could recall, everyone seemed to have hopes that their imprisonment was temporary, and that somehow they'd soon be released. Since they were in an unfamiliar region, language would have been a barrier even if they had been successful in escaping from the concentration camp. There were always many armed guards seen inside and around the barbed wire perimeter of the concentration camp.*

* * * * * * * * * * * * * * * * * *

EDITOR NOTE: *At the beginning of the Wittmans' imprisonment in the Swilara, the officials allowed outsiders to drop off food for the prisoners. When Uncle Andreas discovered where they had become detained, he regularly supplied flour to a nearby bakery for making bread. He asked Joseph Metzger, a fifteen-year-old boy from a Nazarean family to pick up the bread from the bakery and deliver the large loaf to the Wittmann families at the Swilara. Margaretha states that it was a highlight for the first child to spot Joseph through the barbed wire fence. They were so very appreciative and thankful for the bread he brought for them. Then, all at once the officials stopped any items from entering the camp, and that's when the deaths increased dramatically.*

17

Kinder Kamp
January 1946

C ousin Florina died on January 6. Soon after her death, all of the children from the Swilara were ordered to line up. Margaretha was very sick with a fever, but mustered enough energy to stand close to her siblings and cousins. What was in store for them next? Up until now the corporal's ideas and commands only brought more pain and terror. A few mothers were selected to gather with the group of children. Thankfully Mame was one of those selected mothers!

The large group of children and mothers were marched across the Swilara concentration camp, and past the main guard. They walked further along the city road before arriving at another old building referred to as the Kinder Kamp. Inside, rows of wooden boards in two layers served as make-shift bunk beds. No kitchen. No table or chairs. No signs of anything that resembled a home.

There were some children who had already been living inside the building prior to their arrival. Most of them appeared very weak and sickly, and their shallow faces reflected their pain. A few chatted idly, but most of them sat in miserable-looking huddles, attempting to stay warm.

Margaretha didn't remember much after that. As her fever rose, she became more and more delirious. It was almost two weeks before her fever finally broke. At first she was unable to grasp where she was. She couldn't even recall making the original trek from the Swilara concentration camp to the Kinder Kamp.

* * * * * * * * * * * * * * * * * * *

Mame was among the eight random women assigned to care for over a hundred children. Whenever the shrill mealtime bell rang, two of the women would walk to the Swilara to get food. This was no small task for the sickly women. First they carried a big kettle to one of the guards who let them out of the Kinder Kamp. Then they hurried to the Swilara concentration camp to stand in the food line. The trip back was even more exhausting because they had to balance the filled kettle between them.

The soup in the kettle that the women brought back to the Kinder Kamp didn't even begin to satisfy the children's empty tummies. After it was eaten, a few boys hungrily licked out the kettle with hopes of getting just a few more drops. With so little to eat or drink, the children rarely needed to urinate. But if they did, a ditch behind the Kinder Kamp building was used for that purpose.

Mame was always one of the women who volunteered to make the difficult trips to the Swilara for food. She looked for every opportunity to see Tate or Fritz, or find out any tidbit of news about their relatives. But Mame had to be discreet, even in making eye contact with Tate or Fritz.

Sometimes Mame and the other woman were too weak to carry the kettle, so they dragged it behind them. And when they finally returned to the Kinder Kamp, Mame's face would appear even more hollowed than when she left. Margaretha often wondered if it was from the physical strain of the task, or if it was from other things that she may have encountered along the way.

The days at the Kinder Kamp were long and drawn out. There was simply nothing to do besides waiting for the kettle of food to be brought in. At night, they all laid perpendicularly along the parallel rows of long boards. Margaretha learned to turn over slowly. If she wiggled too much, she would get pinched between the shifting boards.

One day the kettle of soup that was brought into the Kinder Kamp had beets in it .... not the red beets that humans eat, but a different kind of beet. Back in Neu Pasua, Margaretha remembered feeding the large, turnip-shaped beets to the cows to help increase their milk production. The beet soup wasn't distasteful, but it didn't take long for everyone at the Kinder Kamp to realize that it gave them severe diarrhea.

* * * * * * * * * * * * * * * * * *

One evening after the soup was distributed and eaten, Mame collapsed onto her bed. Margaretha lay down beside her—almost afraid to ask, but eager to know if she'd seen Tate or Fritz. "I saw Fritz today," Mame mumbled as if even speaking took effort. "He and Jakob are working over there." Mame pointed in the direction of the Swilara concentration camp.

Margaretha waited for Mame to catch her breath. "Sometimes the boys have to go down to the Sava River," Mame continued. "When the boats arrive with the wood, they must go into the river to get the wood from the boats .... poor boys," she murmured. "They go into the water during this freezing winter weather .... with no dry clothes to change into when they get back to the Swilara .... and hardly any food to eat!"

Mame was trembling. Margaretha sensed that there was something more. She wasn't sure if Mame was too troubled or too weak to talk.

"Another one of Fritz's jobs is to ...." Mame hesitated, and cast her eyes downwards before continuing, ".... to pick up the dead bodies. He and another boy have to load the dead bodies on a cart and wheel them over to the big hole."

Margaretha shivered involuntarily. The ghastly sight of the big hole could not be erased from her mind. She despised the corporal and his merciless and sadistic actions. How awful for Fritz to have to touch those dead bodies! It hurt her to see Mame looking so sad. Margaretha gently put her arm around

Mame to comfort her, but she nearly drew back from the sharpness of the bones that she felt under her thin dress. It was during such conversations that Mame would usually end with the same words, "Gretle, if I die ...."

Margaretha didn't want to hear those words, but Mame was insistent. "Gretle, if you ever get out of here, be sure to go to the Nazarean Church and follow the Lord. And let Aunt Eva know that we starved to death."

* * * * * * * * * * * * * * * * * * *

When Mama came back to the Kinder Kamp with the kettle of food one day, Margaretha could tell right away that something was very wrong. "Gretle, I have to go back to the Swilara concentration camp," Mame said breathlessly. "I . . . I got caught doing something, and the main guard said I must report back immediately."

"Don't go!" Margaretha pleaded. She had heard of others suffering terrible punishments under the corporal's directions. She couldn't bear the thought of Mame being whipped, or confined, or . . . would Mame even get to return to the Kinder Kamp, or would she be so cruelly punished that she would die? "Don't go, Mame! Please, don't go," Margaretha begged.

"Gretle," Mame soothed, "you know it will be worse for me if I don't report back. Now take good care of Jakob, Florina, Magdalena, and Herta. And Gretle, if I die, be sure to go to church and follow the Lord. And let Aunt Eva know that we starved to death."

Margaretha couldn't bear to watch Mame leave. She waited anxiously all day and into the night. It wasn't until the wee hours of the next morning when Margaretha finally saw Mame limping back to their Kinder Kamp. What a scare!

* * * * * * * * * * * * * * * * * * *

On January 21, 1946, there was the most terrible news—Margaretha's beloved Tate died. Margaretha hadn't seen Tate since November, and she couldn't quite grasp the fact that she would never see him again for as long as she lived. How sad and helpless she felt. It seemed like an eternity since her happy carefree days back in Neu Pasua. And then there was more bad news; Cousin Liese's father died on January 26

* * * * * * * * * * * * * * * * * * *

EDITOR NOTE: Years later, Margaretha found out from one of her aunts that Mame had purchased some whiskey from a restaurant. Mame and the other woman who helped her carry the food kettle passed a restaurant as they made their way to and from the Swilara. Mame had been suffering from severe burning in her stomach, and hoped that the whiskey would serve as a remedy. She most likely had typhus, a bacterial disease spread by lice which causes severe abdominal pain and inflammation of the stomach.

Margaretha has no idea how Mame would have obtained money to purchase the whiskey but she remembered that Uncle Andreas had given them money back at Velika Pisanica. Somehow she must have kept the money from being discovered during the initial search when they entered the Swilara concentration camp in Mitrovica.

Unfortunately, on the day that Mame got back to the main camp with the whiskey, she had encountered a heartless guard. After the guard had interrogated her, he ordered her to take the filled kettle back to the Kinder Kamp and then report back immediately for her punishment. Her punishment ended in a severe whipping.

18

More Deaths and Despair
February – March 1946

Life was so difficult, and even more so for Mame. On a daily basis she had to witness the destitute condition of her children, relatives, and fellow prisoners. She herself was so very weak and frail. There appeared to be no hope of ever getting out of the concentration camp, and so Mame clung onto the only real hope she had. She shared with Margaretha about eternal life, a promised life in heaven with no more death, pain, or suffering.

Much to the delight of Cousin Liese, Katharina, Johann, and Barbara, their mame, Aunt Elisabeth, was brought to the Kinder Kamp to replace one of the women who had died. Mame also felt some relief in knowing that Aunt Elisabeth would keep an eye on her little ones as she made her daily treks to the Swilara for food.

One day Margaretha overheard Mame telling Aunt Elisabeth that she had seen Cousin Jakob. Jakob, like his father, had stood by the fence that separated the men from the women. He had been very angry as he pounded the fence with his fists. "I have to die! Because of those lies, I have to die!" he had shrieked. On February 3, news spread that Jakob died.

* * * * * * * * * * * * * * * * * *

There was a Serbian woman from the Nazarean Church who lived in Mitrovica. Somehow word had spread to Mame that Aunt Florina had delivered food to the Serbian woman's house. Communication most likely happened during one of

Mame's treks to the Swilara concentration camp for food, or on her return trip back to the Kinder Kamp.

Mame was desperate to keep her children alive. She began sneaking out from the Kinder Kamp to the Serbian woman's house for food whenever she got a chance. Mame wanted Aunt Elisabeth to take turns as well, but Aunt Elisabeth told Mame that she was too fearful of getting caught and the consequences it might bring.

Whenever Mame brought back food from the woman's house, she divided it not only among Margaretha and her siblings, but also among the other hungry children. But no matter how much food she brought back, it was never enough. Margaretha's little sister Magdalena often refused the portion of food that Mama gave her. She'd say, "No, Mame, you need it. You can have it."

On February 27, Mame heard the dreaded news that Fritz had died. In only three more days, Fritz would have turned sixteen years old. The emotional anguish of both Tate's and Fritz's deaths was almost more than Margaretha could bear. Mama was also very distraught, and the horrible conditions that continued inside the Kinder Kamp were no comfort.

* * * * * * * * * * * * * * * * * *

Food was foremost in the children's minds. Starvation not only took away their strength, but it made them irritable and caused them to clamor like animals at any sight of food. While sitting around one day, a child suddenly burst out, "My mame used to make the best baked chicken."

One child added, "We had fresh bread at my house, and my mame used to put sweet honey on my bread."

"I wish I could have some grapes or some oatmeal," said another small child. Soon more children joined in the conversation. Each child babbled on about their favorite meals.

174

They reminisced about their mothers' freshly baked breads and cakes.

"STOP! Stop it, ALL of you!" The eyes of one of the women were wild with anger as she screamed at the children, "Don't speak another word of . . . another word of THAT!" Even talking about food brought on a savage rage.

After the outburst, the children fell silent. Each mind struggled with its own thoughts and images of food while their empty stomachs gnawed in pain. A few children hadn't taken part in the conversation because they were too weak or dizzy. They were past the point of hunger pains, and it wouldn't be long before they too would die of starvation.

* * * * * * * * * * * * * * * * * *

The children faced a multitude of other miserable conditions besides hunger. The itching from the lice never completely left, and many developed sores. There was no access to water. Since they wore the same clothes for months and months, there was always the reeking smell from their poor hygiene. There were no diapers for the little children, and the diarrhea from the beet soup just added to the disgusting odors. The nights were extremely cold, and frostbite was common. Dead bodies were usually found on a daily basis.

So many children with not enough adults to care for them were packed into one room lined with boards that served as their beds. The few mothers were weak and exhausted. They got irritated with each other too, and it was next to impossible for them to give all the children the physical and emotional support that they needed.

* * * * * * * * * * * * * * * * * *

Ever since Tate and Fritz had died, it seemed that Mame had also lost her will to live. By the end of February, Mame was simply too weak to drag the kettle anymore and her eyesight was rapidly declining. Margaretha even had to assist Mama with eating, and she took over caring for baby Herta.

One evening, a woman asked Mame, "Do you know the hymn, 'My Heavenly Mansion'?"

"Yes, I know it," Mame answered.

"Would you . . . could you . . . sing it?" the woman requested.

Mame nodded and looked to Margaretha for support. It was Mame's favorite hymn, and she knew that Margaretha had learned to sing it with her at the Nazarean Church. Margaretha took a deep breath. She was so overcome with emotion that she could hardly sing, but she wanted to sing beautifully for Mame.

The entire Kinder Kamp was in darkness. There were no candles or lanterns. And their circumstances were as black as the night was dark. In the stillness, only Mame and Margaretha's voices could be heard as they sang softly from a corner of the room. Their singing provided a glimmer of light for the hearts and minds of the women and children. For an instant, they were drawn away from the dreadful physical conditions of the concentration camp to a spiritual realm where Christ, not the corporal, was in charge.

In harmony Mame and Margaretha sang the final verse, *"My heavenly mansion beyond the sky, Where they who enter shall never die; There would I journey this very day, And with my Jesus forever stay."* At that moment, Margaretha sensed that Mame was already walking with Jesus through the valley of the shadow of death.

* * * * * * * * * * * * * * * * * *

During the night, Margaretha was awakened by Florina. "Mame told me to get you. She needs your help!" Mame's voice was barely audible by the time Margaretha reached her side.

"Gretle .... help me .... sit up." Margaretha put her arms behind Mame's shriveled body, and lifted her into a sitting position. "There .... I can breathe a bit better now," Mame sighed. "Thank you, Gretle."

Margaretha layed down beside Mame and fell back asleep. But soon Mame called out again, "Gretle .... help me." Mame had slumped down again, and her breathing had become more shallow and labored. Margaretha helped her to sit up again. And, so, the long night passed.

In the morning, Margaretha got up with the other children. Mame was still sleeping. A little while later, one of the women must have noticed that Mame was sleeping longer than usual. "Gretle," she said. "You'd better check on your Mame."

Margaretha wondered why Mame's arm was turned upwards in such a strange position. She reached out to feel it; her hand was cold and stiff. Then the awful reality struck her. Mame was dead. Margaretha suddenly felt so alone, and then began sobbing uncontrollably. Jakob, Florina, Magdalena, and little Herta began crying too.

Mame was only thirty-seven years old. But on that third day in March,1946, there would be no funeral. And on this side of life, there would be no marker to identify Mame's grave. There was only the cart, the one that came around to pick up the dead bodies.

Dead bodies were no longer being buried in the big hole beside the Swilara concentration camp. That hole had long since been filled with hundreds and hundreds of dead prisoners. Now the bodies were picked up from the camps by a cart, and stacked up on a wagon like logs. They were driven away to be disposed of ... somehow ...somewhere. Mame's body was stacked up with the others' and driven away.

* * * * * * * * * * * * * * * * * * *

"Gretle," one of the women later asked Margaretha, "Is there a Matthias in your family? Your Mame kept calling out that name last night." Margaretha told the women that Uncle Matthias was Mame's younger brother. He was a prisoner in a POW camp, and Mame had often prayed for his release.

Now fourteen-year-old Margaretha was left with the responsibility of caring for her younger siblings: twelve-year-old Jakob, nine-year-old Florina, six-year-old Magdalena , and one-year-old Herta. Herta cried continuously for Mame, and she refused to eat. It didn't matter how much Margaretha or Florina tried coaxing her. The other women even tried to help, but Herta only turned away from them too. It nearly broke Margaretha's heart to hear her longingly calling out, "Mame, Mame, Mame!"

Herta's little body looked pitiful. It was a horrible sight to see her wasting away before their very eyes. She died on March 13, only ten days after Mame had died.

Four months earlier, eight members of the Friedrich Wittmann family had entered the Swilara concentration camp. Now, only four of them remained: Margaretha, Jakob, Florina, and Magdalena. And there appeared to be no hope for their future either.

* * * * * * * * * * * * * * * * * *

EDITOR NOTE: The native Yugoslavians who lived in the homes located on all sides of the Mitrovica concentration camp were certainly aware of the prisoners. The gaunt and withered prisoners wandered about in the fenced-in yards and were in plain view of the Mitrovica residents. But, no matter how aware they were of the horrors taking place inside this concentration camp, they wouldn't have had the power to do anything about it anyway.

* * * * * * * * * * * * * * * * * *

EDITOR NOTE: The "lie" that cousin Jakob cried out about was the false belief that the German-Yugoslavian people were evil and that they needed to be destroyed. Tito's regime had established a resolution that deprived those with German heritage of their human rights through mass liquidations, deportations, and extermination by starvation in forced labor or concentration camps.

(Schmidt)

* * * * * * * * * * * * * * * * * * *

EDITOR NOTE: A Neu Pasuan man who survived the concentration camp told Margaretha that he had been with Fritz when he went about his daily duty of picking up the dead bodies. When Fritz stumbled upon Tate's stiff body, he had screamed out before collapsing. Another boy stepped in to lift Tate's body unto the cart. Tate was forty-one years old when he died, surviving only two months of the dreaded Mitrovica concentration camp.

Cousin Jakob Wittmann (far left) pictured with his
school friends

19

Stinging Nettle
April 1946

Margaretha observed more desolation before her as the deaths continued. Many of the prisoners started retaining fluid. Their legs continued to swell until they eventually burst, and then they died. Others had issues with swelling heads. Their eyes looked ghastly. They were pressed so deeply into their large swollen heads that they couldn't even see out of them.

Margaretha noticed her own legs beginning to swell. As her legs grew bigger, the skin became more taut and shiny. She wondered if her blood had turned into water! Margaretha could press her finger into each leg almost as deep as her finger was long. And when she removed her finger, the hole remained there for awhile.

There was not much that could be done. Margaretha wondered if her legs, too, would continue to swell until they burst. Then her hands and even her eyes began to swell. Before long, she was too ill to even get up.

The only things that changed from day to day were the number of deaths, or the number of new children brought into the Kinder Kamp. It was so sad to see the many lonely children who were torn from their families and sent to the Kinder Kamp. Occasionally another woman would be sent to replace one of the mothers who had died.

It was one of those new women who noticed Margaretha's out-of-control swelling. "Oh, my child," she said with compassion. "If you could just drink some stinging nettle tea, all of that water would drain right out of you."

"Really?" Margaretha thought the news sounded too good to be true.

"Yes, and after you drink the tea, make sure you don't lie down or your lungs will fill up with fluid," the woman instructed. "Sit upright and be sure to keep your legs propped up."

The woman had given Margaretha hope for the future. Then, almost as quickly as she arrived at the Kinder Kamp, she disappeared. She was sent away to a government-operated farm for forced labor.

* * * * * * * * * * * * * * * * * * * *

Margaretha's brother Jakob made his way along the barbed wire fence line to where the woman had told him that the stinging nettle grew. It was not easy to grasp the plants through the fence. He didn't have any scissors or a knife, and the hairs on the stinging nettle leaves were painful when he touched them. Jakob took the stinging nettle plants he had collected and made a tea with them. At this point in time, the Kinder Kamp was sometimes given a small pitcher of water.

After Margaretha drank the stinging nettle tea, she faithfully followed the woman's instructions. She sat upright with her back against the cold wall. "The woman said to prop your legs up," Jakob remembered. Somehow he managed to elevate Margaretha's swollen legs by hoisting them up with his belt.

It wasn't long before Margaretha felt the fluid draining from her body. A couple of the women assisted her to the ditch that served as their toilet. It seemed as though she couldn't stop urinating. After several more days, the fluid had drained completely but it left her skin sagging. The stinging nettle tea had worked! God had provided a miracle!

* * * * * * * * * * * * * * * * * * * *

A doctor of German descent was also a prisoner in the Swilara concentration camp. He lived in the same horrible conditions as everyone else. He was given permission to "treat" the people, although he wasn't given anything to treat them with. His little bag contained only some ashes from a fire. The burnt charcoal seemed to help the diarrhea that was caused from the beet soup.

When the doctor made his rounds at the Kinder Kamp, the women were eager to show him their little miracle girl. "Look at Gretle!" they enthusiastically greeted the doctor. "Her legs were so swollen that they were almost ready to burst. Her brother found some stinging nettle leaves and made a tea from it. She drank it, and now just look at her!"

Margaretha was still too weak to stand, but the women lifted her up for the doctor to see. He was very pleased to see what the stinging nettle tea had done, and suggested that it may help others with the same condition. The doctor said that he would talk to the camp officials about the discovery.

A few days later, Margaretha saw some of the women walking beyond the fence line. They were being closely monitored by the watchful guards who went along. The women brought back handfuls of stinging nettle leaves. The leaves were ground up and cooked in the cornmeal at the Swilara concentration camp. After that, the suffering and deaths caused by the swelling decreased dramatically.

* * * * * * * * * * * * * * * * * *

But other illnesses began to surface. A new group of children were brought to the Kinder Kamp. The mothers soon realized that the children's crying was more than just fear and separation anxiety. The children's faces were covered with red spots, and they all had a fever.

Margaretha realized that none of them were going to survive with only the measly food that they were served. Every green blade of grass or twig within an arm's reach beyond the fence line had already been scavenged by the hungry children. Not even a bird that landed within the confines of the camp ever managed to fly off again; it was quickly caught and devoured.

With each passing day the children grew weaker and more malnourished. Sometimes Margaretha would get so weak from lack of food that she would just simply collapse. There was only one way that she could think of to get more food . . . begging at the nearby homes. Just two days ago, she had found a loose board along the fence. What a perfect escape route!

As the children were wandering aimlessly within the fenced-in yard, Margaretha approached Cousin Johann. He was only seven years old. Margaretha hoped that if she took little Johann with her, the villagers might take pity on him when they saw how skinny his little arms and legs were.

"Johann," Margaretha quietly enticed him. "I have some place to show you!"

Johann looked up with interest. Something new to see would be a pleasant surprise.

"I need you to come very quickly and quietly with me," Margaretha said. "And, we can't let the guard see us."

"What are we going to do?" Johann whispered back apprehensively.

"Just do exactly as I say," Margaretha replied boldly, "and then maybe we'll get some food."

When the other children were sidetracked by a bird that flew by, Margaretha and Johann edged their way towards the fence. Then, cautiously, they made their way to the loose board. Margaretha knew that they had to be fast.

The guardhouse was just around the corner of the Kinder Kamp building. Margaretha could see the man's shadow. When he appeared to be looking in the opposite direction, she pulled back on the loose board. The opening was just enough for her slight body to squeeze through. Margaretha grabbed Johann's little hand through the opening and quickly pulled him behind her. They hid on the other side of the fence until Margaretha felt it was safe to move on.

Margaretha needed to make a decision about which house to knock at. What would the people think? Had they seen other beggars? Would they turn them away—or even worse, turn them in to the authorities?

Margaretha fixed her eyes on a house that had its windows open. She and Johann made their way towards the front porch, and then cautiously climbed up the set of stairs. Margaretha knocked several times on the front door while keeping Johann positioned in front of her.

After what seemed like hours, the door was opened partway by a short elderly woman. Prompted by Margaretha, Johann extended his arms while cupping his tiny little hands together. There was nothing they could say that the Serbian woman would understand. The woman babbled in her own language before she motioned the children inside. She quickly shut the door behind them, and led them to her small kitchen.

The woman's kitchen was by no means a luxurious one. But, compared to their awful concentration camp, her kitchen looked cheerful and welcoming. A few cooking supplies were neatly arranged on the wooden shelves above the cooking stove.

When the woman handed Margaretha a loaf of bread, she could hardly take her eyes off of it. A whole loaf—more than she had even hoped for! "Oh, thank you, thank you!" Margaretha stammered. The Serbian woman smiled and nodded.

The trek back to the Kinder Kamp was even more frightful. How would Margaretha know when it would be safe to get past the guard? Getting caught would bring serious consequences for them both.

When she and Johann neared the Kinder Kamp, Margaretha glanced anxiously towards the guardhouse, looking for any sign of the guard. When she finally caught sight of him, he appeared to be looking right at them. They stood frozen in their tracks.

Slowly and deliberately the guard turned his head away from them. Margaretha was so sure that he had seen them. Maybe he had an ounce of compassion and decided to show them mercy. What a relief when they stepped through the opening of the fence and were back inside the Kinder Kamp yard.

Margaretha and Johann crouched themselves down behind the building. They broke off several modest portions to share with their families. Then she and Johann ravenously devoured the rest of the loaf.

Even with the extra bites of food, Margaretha worried about six-year-old Magdalena. It had all started when she developed a fever, and then the dreaded red spots appeared. The Kinder Kamp women were certain that it was the measles.

Margaretha tried her best to care for Magdalena, but there was very little that she could do. Magdalena's inadequate clothing wasn't nearly enough to keep her chilled little body warm. Even though Margaretha begged at the homes in Mitrovica whenever she got an opportunity, there was never enough food or water to give her.

Eventually Magdalena's fever subsided, but by then the poor child was anorexic. How pathetic it was to see her frail body of just skin and bones. She had once been such an energetic and joyful child.

* * * * * * * * * * * * * * * * * * *

EDITOR NOTE: Stinging nettle is a perennial plant that originated in northern Europe and Asia but is now found throughout the world. The plants grow 2 – 4 feet high, and the growing season is between June and September. The leaves and stems of the stinging nettle are covered with tiny hairs that release chemicals and cause pain when coming in contact with skin. However, painful conditions such as muscle and joint pain, eczema, gout, and arthritis have been treated by stinging nettle since medieval times. It is believed that the nettle reduces inflammation and interferes with pain receptors. Available in forms such as extracts, capsules, tea, and topical ointments, stinging nettle has also been used as a diuretic and for treating benign prostatic hyperplasia (BPH). It is recommended that herbs are taken with precautions because they may have side effects or interfere with some medications.

http://umm.edu/health/medical/altmed/herb/stinging-nettle

* * * * * * * * * * * * * * * * * * *

EDITOR NOTE: Margaretha stated it was dangerous for the villagers to extend any help to the concentration camp prisoners. Dire consequences awaited anyone who was discovered getting in the way of exterminating the German population within Yugoslasia. It was also risky for the guards to help the prisoners. Some of the guards weren't as cruel as others, but unfortunately the "good" guards never seemed to stick around for very long.

Photo taken in Neu Pasua approximately 1941
Pictured are Uncle Johann's children L – R:
Katarina, Florina, Barbara, Elisabeth (Liese), and Johann Jr.

20

A Little Relief
May – September 1946

In the spring of 1946, the leadership of the concentration camp changed hands. Rather than being under the direction of bitter and deranged Serbian individuals such as the young corporal, the government was now involved. Conditions slowly began to improve. All of the surviving children from the Kinder Kamp were transferred back to the women's quarters at the Swilara.

One morning the children were instructed to form a line. Pails of powder had been brought in by an American relief organization. Several adults tossed the powder over their heads to exterminate the dreaded lice. As the stinky powder trickled down over Margaretha's body, she nearly choked from the dust. But at last there was relief from the constant itching!

Another day Margaretha was surprised to see some women pouring white powder into a container of water and stirring it. She learned that it was powdered milk, a welcomed addition to the dried cornbread. What a treat!

There were not many pleasurable moments for the children living at the cold and dreary Swilara. However, one particular afternoon outing brought a ray of sunshine into their miserable lives. The guards escorted them to the nearby Sava River and let the children splash around in the water.

* * * * * * * * * * * * * * * * * * *

The Yugoslavian government wanted to make some profit from their concentration camp prisoners. All adults—those who could still walk—were sent to area farms for forced labor. The officials also decided that they would send children from ages ten to fifteen to work on the farms. It was rumored that even though there would always be guards nearby, being a slave on the farms was far better than living in the concentration camp. There would be fresh vegetables to eat, and more opportunities to find food.

In a way Margaretha was excited for the chance to get out of the dingy and depressing Swilara. But, on the other hand, she was torn by having to leave nine-year-old Florina and six-year-old Magdalena behind. They would be left in the hands of a few very sickly women, as would any other children who were under ten years old. However, she didn't have a choice in the matter.

Margaretha, Jakob, Cousin Liese, and Cousin Margaretha were among a group of children sent to work at a flax farm. Their job was to snap off the flax stalks, and then put them into bundles. Hour after hour, day after day, they worked. The guard's gun kept them focused on the task at hand. Just as rumored, the best benefit of working on the farms was the food. How Margaretha loved the fresh tomatoes! At night they slept in the barn on top of a haystack.

It began raining one day as Margaretha and the children were busy pulling the flax stalks. At first the sprinkles were a welcomed break, but soon the continuous rain drops on their backs became bothersome. When the rain turned into a heavy downpour, working conditions turned miserable. Margaretha kept her head down as she worked to shield her face from the stinging rain.

Suddenly, Cousin Liese ran to find cover. Margaretha was amazed by Liese's boldness, and wondered what her punishment would be. When the guard did nothing, she and the other children began running for shelter as well. Perhaps the guard didn't appreciate standing out in the rain either.

After about a month of picking flax at the farm, the child laborers were brought back to the Swilara. Margaretha was anxious to see Florina and Magdalena, but poor little Magdalena's health had not improved. Oh, how Margaretha wished there was something that could be done to help her!

* * * * * * * * * * * * * * * * * * * *

EDITOR NOTE: At one point during this time frame, Jakob became deathly sick. He was so sick that the authorities took him and Magdalena to another building. This building was separate from the Kinder Kamp and the Swilara concentration camp. Only the sickest of the sick children were brought there. At this sick house, no one was assigned to take care of the children, and no guards were posted there. Occasionally someone brought them food. Their efforts were futile, however, because the children at the sick house never got better. They just withered away until they died.

Jakob later told Margaretha that when he first got to the sick house, he was appalled at the living skeletons whose ears were paper thin, and who were only a few breaths away from being dead. He had made a willful decision right then and there that he refused to die inside that sick house. Since there weren't any guards posted there, he stayed outside. At night, he slept on the ground under a tree.

There was a graveyard located next to the sick house, and when the people came to the graveyard during the day, Jakob noticed that some of them set food on the gravestones. Even though this Yugoslavian region was experiencing desperate post-war conditions, it must have been a religious custom to bring food to the gravestone of deceased loved ones.

Jakob went into the graveyard during the night to steal food from the gravestones. He also snuck into the peoples' gardens and plucked the fresh tomatoes and vegetables from their stalks. After being at the sick house for a period of time, Jakob's health began to improve.

SECTION FOUR:

Orphanages

21

Debeljaca
October 1946

A large, dark truck pulled up in front of the main entrance of the Swilara concentration camp. Once again the camp officials made an announcement. All of the children who had lost both parents were instructed to form a line beside the truck, which was bound for an orphanage.

Margaretha and Florina huddled with Jakob and Magdalena, who had recently been brought back to the Swilara from the sick house. Not knowing what to think, or how to respond, they stood apprehensively in line while they were being inspected. One of the guards moved slowly down the line, from one child to the next, and scrutinized them from head to toe. He paused deliberately beside little Magdalena. Tapping his index finger on top of her head, he stated emphatically to one of the other guards. "No . . . . Not this one. Too little and sickly. This one's not going in the truck."

Margaretha was sickened by his harsh words. She felt her heart pounding wildly, and she was too distraught to even think. In her mind she had determined that she would NOT leave the Swilara without Magdalena. Margaretha clung to her frail little sister and tried to ignore what the mean man had just said. She hoped desperately for this nightmare to end. For them to have survived under these inhumane conditions was a miracle in itself. No, it was unthinkable to leave her here!

The other children were already loaded in the truck that would take them to the orphanage, but Margaretha stood her ground as she clung tightly to Magdalena. Then the most awful thing happened. The guard forceably pulled her away from Magdalena. Grabbing Margaretha by one arm and one leg, he literally threw her into the back of the truck. She screamed out in distress!

As the truck roared off, Liese cried out, "I'll watch Magdalena for you, Gretle. I'll try to take good care of her!" (Liese was not an orphan because her mother Aunt Elisabeth was still living. She remained at the Swilara concentration camp, along with her sisters and brother.)

Margaretha was exhausted as she lay slumped against the side of the truck. There was no one who could give her the comfort or emotional support that she needed right then. Of all that she had endured, this was by far the most heartwrenching thing she had ever faced. Tate, Mame, Fritz, and Herta were dead, and now she wondered if she'd ever see Magdalena again.

* * * * * * * * * * * * * * * * * * * *

Two years had passed since the October 6, 1944 fleeing day. Margaretha and each of the other orphans inside the truck had endured their own difficult circumstances as refugees. But they all shared the same fate as starving prisoners inside the Swilara concentration camp at Mitrovica.

The big truck that was transporting them to the orphanage had tall sides with a heavy canvas cover. If the older children stretched upwards, they could lift the edges of the canvas to make small openings to peek out. The truck passed through villages as it made its way through the countryside.

Peeking out of an opening, one of the older boys called out excitedly, "We're in Stara Pasua!" There was a heightened awareness among the Neu Pasuan orphans. They knew that Neu Pasua would be the next village that they would pass through on that main road.

As they got closer to Neu Pasua, Margaretha wondered what they would encounter. Would the village still look the same? Would the truck stop there? Would she recognize any faces? Margaretha's mind reminisced about her happy childhood memories in Neu Pasua. She wondered if their kitchen table still looked the same as when they had left the village on fleeing day.

The orphans clamored to the sides of the truck. The older children lifted up the younger ones, for each of them wanted to get a glimpse of Neu Pasua. But the truck only seemed to be driving faster, and all Margaretha could see was a blur of unkempt yards. The truck rambled past Neu Pasua and into the countryside again.

They drove through several other villages before arriving at Debeljaca, a village in the province of Banat. Margaretha wondered what their new home would look like when the truck pulled up to a large, one-story building. As the children wearily climbed out of the truck and entered the orphanage, the evening sky was darkening.

Margaretha noticed that their arrival caused quite a scurry among the orphanage staff. The workers were unprepared for such a large number of children arriving at once. The children were quickly ushered into their sleeping quarters—the staff probably didn't know what else to do with them. Only a few beds were unoccupied. Margaretha, Florina, and cousin Margaretha all climbed into one bed. Jakob, of course, had to sleep in a different room with other boys.

It didn't take long for Margaretha to fall asleep. The rough truck ride to the orphanage had left her completely drained. During the night, though, Margaretha was awakened by a persistent nudge. It was Jakob.

"May I sleep in here? I can't sleep in that other room." He shuddered, then continued, "Those boys ... Well, they're already dead!"

* * * * * * * * * * * * * * * * * * *

The next morning it was discovered that several boys had died during the night. Morning also brought big changes for Margaretha and the new arrivals at the orphanage. First their heads were completely shaved. The orphanage did not want to take any chances of bringing in head lice. Then they were ushered to a row of showers. Besides the swim in the Sava River after the Mitrovica concentration camp became government controlled, Margararetha and the other new orphans did not have a bath the entire time they were imprisoned. Off came the clothes and undergarments that they had worn for a year and three months! All of their old clothes were discarded.

Each of the children was given two uniforms; one dark blue, and the other one gray. The girls' blouses had seams that were sewn just below the waistline and attached to skirts that were made from a thick serviceable material. The boys' uniform looked identical except that the bottom halves of the uniforms were pants instead of skirts. Their hats were shaped like sailboats when they were folded.

The Debeljaca orphanage was run by Serbian matrons. They were very strict, and their mannerisms were rather insensitive. A few women workers of German descent also worked there. They had been brought into the Debeljaca orphanage from various concentration camps to cook, sew, and clean. The German women seemed more empathetic than the Serbian matrons because they came from similar circumstances and shared a common language with the orphans.

Two long tables were positioned in the center of the dining room; one for the boys, and one for the girls. "Don't eat too much—only a little bit at a time!" the German women warned the newcomers. "There will be more food tomorrow," they reminded them. "If you eat too much, you'll get sick. Children have died from eating too much at once."

At mealtimes, Franz Graber, one of the orphanage boys, traditionally stood at the head of the table. All of the orphans were expected to stand with good posture beside their chairs. Then Franz would put his right thumb up to his temple and say, "Za domovina's Tito!"

In response, the children shouted out, "Napret!"

No prayers were said before the meal was served; there was only the chant. Franz was chosen to lead it because he could speak Serbian fluently, having grown up in the Serbian village of Ruma.

After months and months of starvation, it was difficult to comprehend that there really would be enough food again for the next day. Unfortunately, many orphans didn't heed the women's warnings, and they died from overeating.

* * * * * * * * * * * * * * * * * * * *

EDITOR NOTE: The Serbian chant "Za domovina's Tito!" translates to "For the homeland of Tito!" "Nepret" means "Go ahead" or "Yes."

22

Orphanage Life
October – November 1946

L ife at the Debeljaca orphanage was very structured and methodical. Several of the rules included taking daily showers, getting heights and weights measured weekly, and wearing a uniform at all times.

The children were also expected to memorize several Serbian songs. Since most of the orphans didn't speak any Serbian, they felt like they were reciting senseless syllables. Once the children mastered the Serbian songs, they were marched through the village of Debeljaca. Villagers were entertained by the bald-headed, uniformed orphans as they were paraded throughout the village streets.

The marches through Debeljaca became part of the orphanage's daily routine. During one of these marches, Margaretha began feeling sick to her stomach. Even with the improved diet, many of the children still suffered ill effects from their malnutrition.

Back at the orphanage, Margaretha's queasiness had still not let up as the children filed into the dining hall. She wearily took her place and tried to function, despite the nauseous feeling. Drugarica Milena, one of the Serbian matrons, walked directly up to her and unexpectedly gave her cheek a hard, stinging slap! As Margaretha's hat fell to the floor, she realized too late what her error had been. She had forgotten to remove her hat at meal time.

* * * * * * * * * * * * * * * * * *

One of the Serbian songs they learned was modified to include a dance. As 10 girls danced, the other orphans sang the song. Margaretha was one of those dancing girls. When the song was complete, the dancing girls ended up in a position that looked like a five-point star. Five of the girls were the star's points, and five of the girls formed the indents of the star. All of their arms extended to form the sides of the star. While the girls lay in their star position, the other orphans recited a poem.

A teacher from the town was very impressed by the attractive dance. She inquired about getting the orphans to teach it to her students. Margaretha was thrilled to be invited to the school and interact with the other children. Dancing was therapeutic for her because she was able to enjoy the moment and shut out her situation.

* * * * * * * * * * * * * * * * * * *

Rooms were sometimes reassigned at the Debeljaca orphanage. They typically changed when more children were brought in from concentration camps, or if orphans from Debeljaca were sent to other destinations once their health improved. Margaretha was moved to a larger room, the bedroom where Drugarica, the Serbian matron, and other girls her age slept.

On the first night in her new room, Margaretha folded her hands to pray before going to sleep, as she had been taught by her mother. When she had finished praying, she noticed that Drugarica was staring at her with look of stony hatred. After that, Margaretha decided that she would wait to pray until after dark, and when everyone had fallen asleep.

Drugarica had an intense dislike towards Margaretha that never seemed to diminish. And Margaretha wasn't the only one whose life she made miserable. One night, Drugarica brought Franz Graber into their bedroom and forced him to get into bed with her. Franz fought with all his might, and eventually managed to escape from her grasp. The girls were simply horrified!

* * * * * * * * * * * * * * * * * * * *

Due to the bad living conditions the children had endured prior to their arrival at the orphanage, health issues were common. A very contagious eye disease broke out among half of the children. Margaretha and her cousin Margaretha were among those who were infected. A doctor was summoned to check the childrens' eyes and help stop the spread of disease.

It was decided that the infected children would be taken to a temporary sick house. That way, the children with the eye disease could be treated, and it would prevent the other children from contracting the disease. When only one Margaretha Wittmann was announced, Margaretha let Cousin Margaretha be the one go to the sick house. She stayed behind because she feared the thought of being separated from Jakob and Florina.

Whenever the orphanage asked for volunteers to take food to the children at the sick house, Margaretha offered to go. She was very aware that she needed treatment for her eyes too. Each time that she went to deliver food, she asked the women there to give her some eye drops as well.

Unfortunately, decisions at the orphanage were based on convenience, and not on family ties. It wasn't long before Jakob and a few other children were sent off to an orphanage in Paracin, Serbia. Jakob was only thirteen years old. Once again, Margaretha was separated from a sibling.

* * * * * * * * * * * * * * * * * * * *

EDITOR NOTE: At this point, the government had essentially accomplished their purpose of purging the "German" in these young orphans so they could raise them as supporters of Tito.

23

Zagreb and Osijek
December 1946 – April 1947

One morning, a group of girls, including Margaretha, Hilda Neubauer, Eleanor Neubauer, Amy Binder, Susanna Schmidt, and Katie Frei, were summoned to start packing. Four boys were also told to pack up their belongings. It all happened so fast. Margaretha didn't even have enough time to say a proper goodbye to Florina before they were driven away. Her life of constant change and separation seemed neverending.

The orphans were brought to a train station. There they boarded a train that took them to an orphanage in Zagreb, the capital city of Croatia. How surprised Margaretha and the other girls were when they realized that they were the only girls in an orphanage filled with boys!

While living at the Zagreb orphanage, Margaretha got sick and developed a fever. She remembered shaking so uncontrollably that even the bed itself shook underneath her! A doctor was called in to evaluate her condition. He talked with the orphanage staff at her bedside, but Margaretha didn't know what they were saying about her. Fortunately, she recovered fairly quickly from that episode.

Christmas 1946 was approaching, and Margaretha felt so lonely without any family. The orphanage had a Christmas tree. Hilda, Eleanor, Amy, and Susanna all knelt down by the tree as they performed the Catholic cross symbol with their hands. Only Margaretha and Katie remained standing because neither of them had a Catholic background. From that day forward, Margaretha and Katie developed a close friendship.

The girls all had various jobs that they were required to do. One of their tasks was to pair up the boys' socks from the clean laundry. Whenever there was a mismatched sock, the girls would unravel the yarn so that they could knit socks for themselves. All of them had some knitting experience, but only Margaretha knew how to start and finish the socks. Because Margartha was so busy starting and finishing the other girls' socks, she ended up with socks that were different colors.

* * * * * * * * * * * * * * * * * * * *

After several weeks at the Zagreb orphanage, all six of the girls were transferred to an orphanage in Osijek called Djecji Dom Vladimir Nazora. This large orphanage had two buildings; one for the girls, and one for the boys. Margaretha and the other five girls were made to work in the big kitchen of the boy's building. At this point in time, the girls were too old to go to school.

For some unknown reason, one of the women who worked at the orphanage took an immediate dislike to the new German-speaking girls. At mealtimes she would arrange things so that food was withheld from the girls, or make it so that their portions were very limited. Their poor diet caused them to lose weight.

It was Hilda who overheard the conspiracy among the women who worked in the orphanage kitchen. She could understand Serbian because of the time she had spent with a Serbian neighbor while growing up. Eventually the mistreatment of the girls was revealed to the head of the orphanage, and the woman was fired.

One day, the woman who was in charge of the Osijek orphanage approached Margaretha. "I'd like you to clean my room. Do you think you could do a good job?"

"Yes, I'll sure try," Margaretha responded. A strong work ethic had been instilled in her from early childhood.

When Margaretha had finished cleaning the woman's room, it was spotless.

"Very well done," the lady praised her. "Here's a little something for your hard work." She pressed a paper into Margaretha's hand. It was a ticket to a movie.

Margaretha looked forward to going to a movie even if she couldn't understand the language. But the movie turned out to be an anti-German production, and Margaretha was horrified when the movie showed people doing awful things to Hitler's head. She couldn't bear looking at the screen, yet couldn't seem to tear her eyes away from it either. Mame's voice kept echoing in her ears, "It's all because of Hitler that we ended up in this camp."

Back at the orphanage, Margaretha found her head spinning with anxious thoughts, and that evening she had nightmares. The next time the woman gave her a movie ticket for cleaning, she handed it directly to one of the other girls. Margaretha had her fill of watching movies.

Margaretha was so tired of being moved from one orphanage to another. She was very lonesome and longed for family and a normal life. She wondered if Aunt Florina was still living in Beška. She decided to find out, and wrote her a letter. The only thing she remembered was the village name, but it certainly couldn't hurt to try.

* * * * * * * * * * * * * * * * * * * *

What a surprise to receive such a prompt reply to her letter! Margaretha was overjoyed to finally have connections with a family member. Margaretha poured out her heart in a letter to Aunt Florina about how lonely she was. She described all that had happened at the Mitrovica concentration camp, and relayed the deaths of Mame, Tate, Fritz, Herta, and the other relatives. Margaretha expressed how distraught she had been when the concentration camp guard forcibly pulled her away from little Magdalena, and how being separated from Jakob and Florina only made things worse.

Margaretha and Aunt Florina wrote many letters back and forth before the manager of the orphanage approached her. "I would like to see you in my office," he said. Margaretha followed him into his office and wondered if their meeting would lead to a good or bad situation. She was comforted when the man spoke German to her. "I've noticed the many letters that you receive from a woman named Florina who lives in Beška. Who is this woman?"

"She's my aunt," Margaretha replied politely. She hoped that this would not cause any trouble for Aunt Florina.

"I used to be a school teacher in Beška, so I know many of the people from there. I just wondered who this woman was," he continued kindly. "Why don't you write her another letter? Explain to your aunt that if she can obtain papers to prove she can financially support you, then she can be your guardian and get you released from this orphanage."

Be released from the orphanage to live with Aunt Florina? Margaretha couldn't imagine any better news! "Oh, th-thank you, sir," Margaretha stammered. "I'll do that right away!" Margaretha immediately sat down to write Aunt Florina a letter.

* * * * * * * * * * * * * * * * * * *

Every day seemed longer and longer as she anxiously waited for a response. After what seemed like an eternity, Margaretha received the anticipated letter. Aunt Florina was able to obtain the official paperwork to get her released from the orphanage. Finally she could see an end to orphanage life!

May 2, 1947 was a very special day. Because Aunt Florina was not fluent in Serbian, she sent Agnes Kniesel to pick fifteen-year-old Margaretha up from the orphanage. Agnes was the mother of 10 children who had once lived in the

Wittmanns' smaller house on their property in Neu Pasua. Margaretha said her goodbyes to Hilda, Eleanor, Amy, Susanna, and Katie, and looked forward to a new life of freedom.

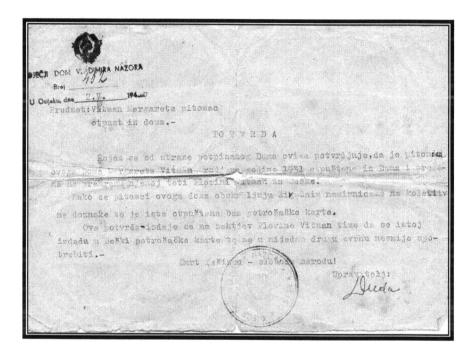

Margaretha's release paper from the Osijek Orphanage

SECTION FIVE:

Living with Aunt Florina

24

Life Outside of the Orphanages
Spring – Summer 1947

W hat a joy it was to escape orphanage life and be reunited with Aunt Florina! She lived in Beška, and Uncle Andreas and Aunt Elisabeth Betsch also lived nearby. Margaretha reminisced about the time when she and Cousin Liese took the train from Neu Pasua to Aunt Florina's house during their summer vacation.

It didn't take long, however, for Margaretha to learn that complete freedom did not exist outside of the orphanage. Communist propaganda was everywhere. Tito was still determined to stamp out any German influence. In civilian raids, the government continued to round up anyone of German descent and put them into concentration camps. The German people had to stay out of the public eye and conduct themselves carefully to avoid appearing "too German."

Aunt Florina owned two cows. "You're nearly sixteen," Aunt Florina reminded Margaretha. "You may get married before too long, and then one of these cows will be yours!" Traditionally, a Neu Pasuan girl received a cow as part of her dowry. There was an old saying in Neu Pasua, "Eine kuh deckt alle armud zu." ("One cow will provide for the poor.")

The postwar Yugoslavian government began controlling property and businesses. According to Tito's five-year plan, it started with the larger farms. The government required a certain percentage of their crops, and sometimes demanded even more than what was harvested. That meant that the owners of the large farms had to buy crops from smaller farms in order to meet their quota.

Life was complicated under the Tito plan, and it was difficult for Aunt Florina and Margaretha to make ends meet. Aunt Florina's farm was considered a large one. When she didn't have enough grain to meet the quota, she had no choice but to sell the two cows in order to buy wheat from a smaller farm. Even that did not satisfy the government's constant demands.

Aunt Florina decided she would go to the city hall and explain her predicament. "Don't leave the house, Gretle," Aunt Florina instructed Margaretha before she left. "And be sure to keep the doors locked." All day long Margaretha was anxious. She feared that she and Aunt Florina would get caught and put into a concentration camp. It was many hours later before Aunt Florina finally arrived back home. Thankfully nothing ended up being out of the ordinary that day.

* * * * * * * * * * * * * * * * * * * *

A Bosnian family gave Aunt Florina their two goats because they didn't have enough hay to feed them over the winter. Aunt Florina's two cows had been sold, but there was still plenty of hay in the barn. Margaretha was excited to have the two goats on their farm. The milk was so rich and creamy, and she especially liked to eat corn cooked with goat's milk and sprinkled with sugar.

Gradually Margaretha began to gain some weight. How grateful she was that she didn't have any more issues with swelling and water retention! She had previously been told by a doctor that she may have problems with swelling for the rest of her life. The goat's milk seemed to be a perfect remedy for poor health.

Adjusting to civilian life was not always easy. Margaretha's hair was still very short and had a disgraceful appearance. She made a habit of wearing a kerchief over her head. That way, even the neighborhood children wouldn't be able to see how bald she really was.

On Sundays Aunt Florina and Margaretha went to the Nazarean Church in Beška. The Kniesels also attended that church. Sunday was the one day of the week that Margaretha could get refreshed and inspired by the truth of the Bible, not weighed down by the propaganda that was infiltrated around her during the rest of the week.

Unfortunately for Margaretha, the Beška Church sermons were preached in Serbian. It was a language that she found very difficult to learn. Whenever the minister read from the Serbian Bible, Margaretha followed along with her German Bible. During the week Margaretha repeatedly asked Uncle Andreas to translate phrases into the Serbian language, and her comprehension gradually improved.

At sugar beet harvest time Margaretha helped Simo Tunic, the minister from their church, at his farm. Two of the Kniesel girls, Laura and Adela, also helped. As the girls hoed the weeds around the beet plants, they chatted and laughed and sang songs. It helped to divert their minds from the endless rows of beets to hoe.

Margaretha began singing one of the Serbian songs that she had learned from the Debeljaca orphanage. She was surprised when the Kniesel girls burst into laughter; she didn't know what was so funny. When the Kniesel girls translated the stanzas, it was Margaretha's turn to laugh. The Serbian song she had just sung was nothing but silly, propaganda phrases.

The orphanage songs made Margaretha think about the lonely times she had there. Even now, so many questions were unanswered. Where were Jakob and Florina? Was Magdalena still alive? Did they all miss her as she missed them? Margaretha wondered if they'd ever see each other again.

* * * * * * * * * * * * * * * * * *

EDITOR NOTE: To this day, Margaretha can still recite some of the Serbian poems and songs that she learned at the Debeljaca orphanage.

25

Troubles with the Government
Fall 1947

In the fall of 1947, Uncle Andreas was petitioned to the city hall. Aunt Elisabeth was afraid to stay home alone that night with her three small children Jakob, Florina, and Reinholdt. At Aunt Elisabeth's request, Margaretha went to stay overnight with her aunt and her cousins. All of them were anxious about what Uncle Andreas would encounter at the city hall, and they all prayed for his safe return.

Uncle Andreas didn't get home until the wee hours of the next morning. But later that day, they were all taken by surprise when two officials showed up at their doorstep. They informed Uncle Andreas and Aunt Elisabeth that they had come to take their family to a concentration camp. Aunt Elisabeth quickly explained that Margaretha was not even one of their children. It seemed like a miracle when the officials gave Margaretha permission to leave, but her heart ached for the overwhelming fear on the faces of the Betsch family.

Margaretha darted across the Betsch's field to Aunt Florina's house as fast as she could. Breathlessly she described to Aunt Florina what had taken place just minutes ago. The two of them put on as many clothes as possible, because they fully expected to be hauled off to the concentration camp as well. They spent the day praying, and had a sleepless night.

As expected, the same two officials pulled into Aunt Florina's yard on motorcycles the very next morning. They poked around inside the farm buildings, and then intrusively stepped into the house. Their first question was directed towards Aunt Florina. "Why don't you have furniture as nice as your sister's?"

Aunt Florina answered their questions as well as she could, and she showed the officials the paperwork from the city hall that declared Margaretha to be a free citizen. Eventually the men left. They left, it seemed, because there were not enough valuable things around their home for them to bother with. However, they did take Aunt Florina's plow as well as a few other small pieces of machinery.

Several days later, Margaretha saw the same two officials driving a beautiful team of horses down their road. As they passed by Aunt Florina's driveway, the horses attempted to turn in. The two men had quite a struggle with the reigns. Somehow they managed to get the horses under control, and they continued trotting down the road.

There was no doubt in Margaretha's mind that they were Uncle Andreas's team of horses, the ones that the officials had confiscated only a few days ago. Aunt Florina's driveway would have been a familiar landmark for the horses because Uncle Andreas and Aunt Elisabeth came over often. The Betsch home had been completely emptied of possessions, and other valuable goods around the farm were also taken.

* * * * * * * * * * * * * * * * * *

How relieved Aunt Florina was when they finally received a letter in the mail from the Betsch family. The letter stated that they had been sent to a concentration camp in Gakova. Immediately Aunt Florina and Margaretha began setting aside food products for a care package.

Uncle Andreas's brother-in-law Johann arranged a trip to Gakova that he and Margaretha took together. The first part of their journey was by train, and it was in such poor condition that it didn't even have seats for them to sit on. But their physical discomfort seemed trivial compared to the Betsch family's imprisonment inside the Gakova concentration camp.

When they got to the concentration camp, they weren't permitted to see the Betsch family. The main guard accepted their labeled package, and then they were forced to leave. There was simply nothing else they could do. Disappointed, the two of them travelled back to Beška again.

* * * * * * * * * * * * * * * * * * *

Margaretha took another trip with Aunt Florina. Their mission was to find the concentration camp in Jarak. Cousin Liese and her family had endured another winter in the Mitrovica concentration camp before being transferred to Jarak. Margaretha and Aunt Florina took the train as far as the city of Ruma.

In Ruma, they had to take a horse and buggy taxi to Jarak. An acquaintance had suggested that Aunt Florina and Margaretha stay overnight at the home of a widow they knew who lived in the area. The old woman was very kind and hospitable, but Margaretha didn't sleep a wink that night. Fleas were literally jumping around on her blanket!

The next morning, Margaretha and Aunt Florina continued in their search to locate the concentration camp. When they finally found it, they encountered guards like the ones at the Gakova concentration camp. They weren't allowed to see their relatives, but the guards let them drop off some blankets and a food package labeled for the Wittmann family.

* * * * * * * * * * * * * * * * * * *

Weeks later Margaretha took another trip to the Jarak concentration camp by herself. Before leaving on the train, she emphatically told Aunt Florina that she refused to stay overnight at the widow's house in Jarak. But by the time Margaretha arrived there with the horse and buggy taxi, she changed her mind. She simply didn't know where else she could sleep that night. And, just like before, there were fleas jumping around on her blanket!

Besides delivering the food package to the Jarak concentration camp, Margaretha was able to locate Cousin Liese. She had been sent to work on a watermelon farm on the outskirts of the village of Jarak. Liese and a Serbian girl from the village were assigned to watch over the melon field. Whenever any birds came near the melons, the girls' job was to ring bells to scare them away.

Margaretha and Liese had so much to talk about. Liese had tried her best to care for poor little Magdalena after the truck had taken Margaretha and the other orphans away. Margaretha sobbed as Liese described how the starvation continued, and how Magdalena's knees and joints began to bulge. Then her eyes began to swell, and her face became more hollowed. There was simply nothing that Liese could do. Magdalena died only a few weeks later.

Liese was thankful for the opportunity to be on the farm, a much better environment than living at the dreary Swilara in Mitrovica. She only had one request for Margaretha if she ever had the chance to see her again. She hoped for newspaper to use as toilet paper. Cornstalks were the only thing available to wipe with, and the stalks were so rough that they caused sores.

The next day was Sunday, when no one was required to do any work. While working with the Serbian girl from Jarak, Liese had discovered that they were both from Nazarean families. The Serbian girl invited Liese and Margaretha to go to church with her. The small congregation warmly welcomed the girls to their church service. Then, all too soon, it was time for Margaretha to head back to Beška.

* * * * * * * * * * * * * * * * * * *

A train stopped in Beška later that fall. The passengers were concentration camp prisoners who were being transferred to a forced labor camp. At the station, the prisoners were permitted to get off the train to beg food from the villagers.

Since Aunt Florina's house was not far from the train station, some of the prisoners came knocking at their door. Margaretha was the only one at home at the time because Aunt Florina was away delivering another care package to the Betsch family. As Margaretha listened to the prisoners' pleading for food, she remembered so clearly how she and little cousin Johann had snuck out of the Kinder Kamp to beg at the villagers' homes. It felt strange to be on the other side of the picture, and she didn't hesitate to give them whatever food they could spare.

The train prisoners were encouraged to discover someone who was not only sympathetic, but who could also speak German. Margaretha shared with the prisoners how she had survived the Mitrovica concentration camp, and how she had become a free citizen.

One of the prisoners introduced himself as Mr. Kittelberger. He asked Margaretha if she knew of any Nazarean believers who lived in Beška. He was surprised to learn that Margaretha attended the Nazarean Church in Beška. Mr. Kittelberger inquired about an older gentleman named Jakob Betschel. Margaretha was more than happy to lead Mr. Kittelberger past their backyard garden to his friend's house.

After Mr. Kittelberger left, another prisoner knocked on the door. Fortunately, Aunt Florina had a full crock of sauerkraut in the pantry. Margaretha was happy to give the prisoner a generous portion. Word must have quickly spread among the other prisoners because it didn't take long before more of them arrived at her doorstep begging for sauerkraut. Soon the crock of sauerkraut was completely emptied. Margaretha felt bad when she had to turn some of them away empty-handed.

Now there wasn't any more sauerkraut left, and most of their other food was gone too. Margaretha worried about what

Aunt Florina would say when she got back. She knew that food was not plentiful for herself and Aunt Florina either, but she had empathized with the starving train prisoners.

When Aunt Florina arrived back home, Margaretha told her about the begging train prisoners. She confessed about giving away the sauerkraut and almost all of their food. How relieved she was when Aunt Florina said, "Well, Gretle, you did the right thing."

* * * * * * * * * * * * * * * * * * *

Farming became more difficult for Aunt Florina and Margaretha. It was stressful trying to meet the frequent demands of grain for the government. Aunt Florina felt almost relieved when the Yugoslavian government made a decision to confiscate her land. Now they both became government employees.

Margaretha's government job was to milk six cows by hand. Every morning and evening Margaretha walked three kilometers to and from a newly constructed government barn. On Sunday mornings she covered her head tightly with a kerchief to keep out the odor. After milking the cows, she would hurry home. There was just enough time to quickly change, freshen up, and then head to church to be on time for the service.

A dressmaker named Edushka gave Margaretha some sewing lessons between her milking hours. Fees were usually charged for sewing lessons, but Edushka agreed to give her free lessons because she was an orphan. Margaretha soon learned that the lessons weren't really for free. It seemed that Edushka arrived at Aunt Florina's house whenever there were freshly made doughnuts or other baked goods. And Edushka liked to eat her fill!

Lessons with Edushka went well. She was a good instructor and was amazed at how fast Margaretha learned.

Often, after cutting out sleeves from the material, Edushka would say, "Gretle, you sew these together. You do a better job than me!"

* * * * * * * * * * * * * * * * * * *

The government continued to train more milkmaids, and after some time passed Margaretha got a new job. Her assigned government job was to deliver milk to houses with a horse and a wagon. The milk was stored in large tin containers.

One Serbian woman who lived along her milk route expected to have her milk delivered first. Whenever the Serbian woman's children saw Margaretha and her horse and wagon nearing their house, they would invariably shout out, "Here comes the milk lady, the milk lady!" She detested being called "the milk lady."

Margaretha was anxious during her milk route because she'd never know when her horse would have its occasional seizure-like episodes. It always started when the horse began twitching nervously, and then it would get down on its knees and shake uncontrollably. This created problems, especially when they were going uphill because the wagon would start rolling backwards! It got to a point where Margaretha was just too fearful to do her milk route. She decided to inquire about getting a different job.

Aunt Florina accompanied Margaretha to the government office. She also hoped to do something else because her job of picking vegetables was becoming increasingly more difficult for her physically. As they began explaining their situations, the government official turned his attention towards Margaretha. "Why wouldn't you want a nice job like delivering milk?" he stated.

"Oh, I'd rather have a job picking vegetables," Margaretha responded. It turned out that the two of them were able to switch roles. The government official gave Aunt Florina the job of delivering milk, and Margaretha was assigned to a large collective farm as a vegetable picker. At times she even worked on the same land that Aunt Florina had previously owned. She was also given the responsibility of feeding and caring for hundreds of rabbits and chickens and gathering the eggs.

* *

EDITOR NOTE: In a February 1991 article written in The Heimatbote, *Frank Schmidt brings to light a media cover-up ignoring the ethnic cleansing, which includes the atrocity of the Danube Swabians (1944–1948). He states that the Swabians "became scapegoats who bore the brunt of the hatreds against all things German." (Schmidt)*

Margaretha and her siblings were among approximately 40,000 orphans who were removed from the concentration camps by the government and taken to orphanages to become Tito supporters. Schmidt estimates that there were about 1.6 million Danube Swabians who had migrated to Austria, Yugoslavia, Hungary, and Romania. Approximately 200,000 Swabians in Yugoslavia alone were murdered, seized for forced labor, or starved and mistreated in concentration camps. (Hudjetz-Loeber)

As told to Margaretha in personal accounts by other survivors, entire villages were made into concentration camps by the Communists. Many Danube Swabians were trapped in their own villages because burned bridges prevented them from fleeing.

26

Happy Reunions
1950 – 1951

Time passed in Beška, Yugoslavia. Then Aunt Elisabeth Wittmann and cousins Liese, Katarina, Johann, and Barbara were eventually freed from the Jarak concentration camp. They had also made connections with Aunt Florina, and she welcomed them all warmly into her home.

How excited Margaretha and Liese were to be reunited! Both girls were assigned to work at a large government farm. Their job wasn't easy. First they had to load a wagon with heavy feed bags at a feed mill. Then they drove the team of horses with the full wagonload to a pig farm, where they unloaded the feed bags. By the time the girls returned home each evening, they smelled just like the pigpens that they worked in!

Aunt Florina didn't think it was appropriate for the girls to be doing such hard and dirty work. She most certainly didn't appreciate the swine stench either. But the girls didn't have any say because that was the job that the government officials had assigned to them.

* * * * * * * * * * * * * * * * * * *

A very special letter arrived in the mail. The letter was from Jakob, Margaretha's brother! Margaretha was amazed that Jakob had even remembered the village name of Beška. In the letter, Jakob inquired if Aunt Florina still lived there. If so, he hoped to obtain a permission slip from his orphanage in Paracin to visit her during his vacation.

Aunt Florina, of course, quickly replied to Jakob's letter. She let him know that Margaretha and Aunt Elisabeth and her children were all living with her, and that everyone was anxious to see him. After the letter was sent off, Margaretha could hardly contain her emotions—how she longed to see Jakob again! She thought about him constantly while she went about her daily job of hauling feed bags. She wondered what he looked like and what he'd done over the past few years while living at the orphanage.

Jakob sent them another letter stating that the orphanage granted his vacation request, and that he had obtained the official paperwork for his visit. Margaretha was ecstatic, and every day seemed longer and longer as she anticipated Jakob's arrival.

Then—even before Jakob was scheduled to come to Beška—Margaretha discovered news about her sister Florina! The news came about from a letter that Cousin Margaretha wrote to some relatives. According to the letter, she and Florina were both living in a Slovenian orphanage near the Austrian border.

* * * * * * * * * * * * * * * * * * *

It was a bittersweet reunion at the train station—so much of the joy in seeing Jakob mixed with the sorrow and suffering they had endured together. Jakob looked so thin and frail. Margaretha began crying so hard that it felt like a dam had just broken loose. So many emotions had been penned up inside of her.

"Oh, please don't cry so!" Jakob exclaimed in a foreign tongue.

Margaretha was surprised to hear Jakob speaking in Serbian. Apparently he had been exposed solely to the Serbian language over the past few years while living at the Paracin orphanage. He barely remembered any German words. Their communication was less than ideal.

It was evening by the time the three of them arrived at the house. They removed their shoes at the porch entrance, and then Aunt Florina and Margaretha ushered Jakob into the living room. Aunt Elisabeth and the cousins crowded around him because they were all excited to see him and hear about his orphanage experiences. Jakob responded to their questions in Serbian.

Jakob shared that there were about 280 boys living with him at the Paracin orphanage. He had attended a Serbian school there and learned the trades of furniture making and glasswork. When the orphanage discovered how good he was with numbers, they put him to work as a clerk in a general store that sold everything from fabric to hardware and groceries. Jakob was also entrusted with bringing the money from the store to the bank.

After working as a store clerk for some time, Jakob also began wondering how he could make connections with family. He remembered only that Aunt Florina lived in the village of Beška. How amazed he had been when he discovered that his letter actually got delivered to Aunt Florina, and now he was standing in the midst of them all!

Aunt Florina was especially concerned about his health, his diet, and his living conditions. She wondered if the orphanage provided him with a good pair of shoes to wear. "Oh, I have excellent shoes!" he quickly replied in Serbian.

All too soon it was time for the happy household to retire for the night. Today had been very special—a day that Margaretha would remember for a very long time. But with such a tumble of emotions, it was difficult for Margaretha to get to sleep that night. Jakob's presence also reminded her of Tate, Mame, Fritz, Magdalena, and little Herta, her family members whose lives had been cruelly snuffed out at the Mitrovica concentration camp. And how she ached to see Florina!

The next morning Margaretha got up early. It was almost like a dream that Jakob was really there with her in person. Despite the language barrier, Margaretha and Jakob continued to catch up on each other's lives. They discussed the possibility of traveling to Slovenia to see Florina. Since she was only about fourteen years old at this point in time, it would be unlikely that her orphanage would give her permission to leave.

Aunt Florina helped Margaretha and Jakob make travel plans to Slovenia. It wouldn't be an easy trip—they would have to travel over 500 kilometers by train. Margaretha would need to get permission for time off from her job, and she and Jakob would have to come up with the money that they needed for traveling.

Their conversation was interrupted by Liese's laughter as she brought in Jakob's shoes from the porch. It turned out that Jakob's shoes weren't "excellent" by any means. Both shoes had very little sole left, and they barely held together. Margaretha and Aunt Florina must have been so excited to see Jakob at the train station the previous day that they didn't look down at his feet. Then everyone—including Jakob—laughed at the contrariness of his statement. Apparently, his "excellent" meant that he was content with his shoes.

* * * * * * * * * * * * * * * * * * *

As soon as Margaretha got permission for a leave from her job, she and Jakob began preparing for their trip to visit Florina. They packed clothes and food for the journey, and Aunt Florina brought them to the train station. Margaretha felt excited yet apprehensive at the same time. It had been several years since she had last seen Florina. So many unanswered questions flooded her mind as she and Jakob boarded the train headed to Gornja-Radgona.

226

Once Margaretha and Jakob got to Gornja-Radgona, they sought out local people to inquire about the location of the orphanage. Thankfully, even though Gornja-Radgona was a Slovenian village, some of the villagers could understand a little German and Serbian. They were directed to a large hillside building. From a distance, Margaretha thought that the orphanage building looked like a castle.

Many questions filled Margaretha's and Jakob's minds as they made their way up the hill to Florina's orphanage. It had been so long since the three of them had been together at the Debeljaca orphanage. Would they recognize Florina? More importantly, would she recognize them?

Margaretha and Jakob walked into the inner courtyard of the orphanage and looked about them. They expected to see some children about, but the courtyard was deserted. They knocked on the door, and a tall, matronly woman opened it. "We are here to see Florina Wittmann," Margaretha inquired.

"Sorry, none of the children are here. During the summer months we send them away to work on farms," the kind woman explained. She gave Margaretha and Jakob an address to the farm where Florina was working. Unfortunately, the farm was several kilometers away from the orphanage. Even though Margaretha and Jakob were weary from traveling, they determined that they would not give up until they saw Florina.

After Margaretha and Jakob walked for some time, they finally spotted an apple orchard in the distance. According to the woman from the orphanage, it was the landmark to watch for. As they drew nearer, they saw a young girl who looked like their sister, sorting apples into bushel baskets. Margaretha and Jakob broke into a run.

It really was Florina! At first, she had a puzzled look on her face as Margaretha and Jakob came running towards her. Then she shouted excitedly when she recognized her siblings! They all hugged each other, and cried out in their joyfulness.

The three of them quickly realized that their communication was nearly impossible. At the orphanage, Florina had learned Slovenian. Like Jakob, Florina had spoken very little German over the last few years. And the Slovenian language was entirely different from German and Serbian.

As the three siblings sat on the ground under the shade of the apple trees, they stumbled over words that seemed to make no sense to each other. The language barrier was too much, and so they just sat there and cried. How confusing life was! And what an overwhelming flow of emotions they each had!

Margaretha was surprised when she found out that the Slovenian farmer could speak some German. The kind man tried his best to translate Margaretha's and Jakob's questions into Slovenian for Florina, and then translated Florina's responses into German. Florina shared how she and Cousin Margaretha had pretended to be sisters while they were living together at the Slovenian orphanage. Cousin Margaretha had recently been sent off to another orphanage.

Margaretha treasured each moment that the three of them had together because she knew that their time was limited. All too soon, a few days later, it was time for Jakob and her to leave. Maybe next summer Florina would be old enough to spend her holiday with them in Beška.

Photo taken in Beška, 1952
Back Row: Katharina and Liese Wittmann,
Jakob and Margaretha Wittmann
Middle Row: Barbara Wittmann, Aunt Elisabeth Wittmann,
Aunt Florina Wittmann,
Aunt Elisabeth Betsch, Reinhold Betsch, Uncle Andreas Betsch,
Florina Betsch
Front Row: Johann Wittmann, Jakob Betsch

Uncle Jakob Wittmann's two daughters Margaretha (far left) and Elisabeth (far right), pictured with two unidentified boys. This photo was takin in Austria before the girls entered the concentration camp. Cousin Margaretha survived the concentration camp and was the key to helping Margaretha and Jakob find their sister Florina.

L-R: Liese, Barbara, and Margaretha
Photo taken while working at the government farm.
The boy at the back of the wagon is unidentified.

SECTION SIX:

Immigrating

27

Germany
1952

During the summer of 1952, Jakob was released from the Paracin orphanage. He came to live with Aunt Florina and the rest of the household living in Beška. Aunt Florina traveled to the Slovenian orphanage and brought Florina back with her. When Florina arrived, Margaretha surprised her with matching dresses that she had sewed for just the two of them. Jakob, Margaretha, and Florina were inseparable during Florina's short visit.

After Florina left, Margaretha and Liese worked hard at their government farm job. They were elated when they found out that they would be granted some vacation time. The two of them began saving their money to go to Dubronik, a city located near the ocean. Margaretha and Liese could hardly wait!

Just before their vacation drew near, an unexpected letter arrived from Mame's twin brother Jakob Deschner. Uncle Jakob and Uncle Mattias Deschner had both moved to Germany after they were released from their POW camps. Uncle Jakob wrote that he wanted Margaretha and Jakob to be free citizens. He had petitioned for them to immigrate to Germany to live with him, and now their applications had been accepted!

Traveling was expensive, and there wouldn't be enough money for a vacation and a trip to Germany. Margaretha was left with no choice. She had to back out of her plans to go to Dubronik. Liese, of course, was disappointed but she managed to find another girl to go along with her.

* * * * * * * * * * * * * * * * * * *

Margaretha took a train to Belgrade. She went to the German Council to get the required paperwork for her and Jakob to travel to Germany, and then she returned to Beška. The paperwork would serve as identification to show the border patrols as they crossed into Germany.

On the 25th of November, Aunt Florina and Cousin Liese traveled to the train station in Belgrade with Margaretha and Jakob to see them off. Through tearful goodbyes, Aunt Florina gave Margaretha and Jakob their own bowl and spoon. She told them they'd most likely need them at the border crossing camp.

The train stopped in Piding, the crossing camp at the German border. Margaretha and Jakob showed the German patrols their Yugoslavian identification passbooks as well as their Germany acceptance papers from Belgrade. They stood in lines while they waited for health inspections that included lice checks and X-rays. Thank goodness Aunt Florina had the insight to send them off with the bowls and spoons! The utensils were invaluable for the soup lines. Two days later, on November 27, they got the paperwork to travel on to the province of Bayern in southern Germany.

As Margaretha and Jakob boarded another train, they showed the conductor the piece of paper that had Uncle Jacob Deschner's town, Lantendorf, written on it. As there was no train station in Lantendorf, the conductor kindly stopped the train for them as close to the village as possible. When Margaretha and Jakob got off the train, it seemed as though they were in the middle of nowhere. Holding on to their few belongings, they began their trek towards the town.

The first person they came across during their walk was a kind farmer. It turned out that he knew exactly where Uncle Jakob lived, and his directions were easy to follow. They were much relieved when they finally reached Uncle Jakob's house.

It was another bittersweet moment. Even though Margaretha and Jakob felt such joy in seeing their Uncle Jakob,

236

he also vivdly reminded them of Mame. As Mame's twin brother, he not only looked like her, but he also had some of her mannerisms.

Uncle Jakob was delighted to have his niece and nephew living with him. Unfortunately, it turned out that there were no employment opportunities in the rural farming region. Even though Margaretha appreciated Uncle Jakob's kindness, she really missed the weekly fellowship that she received from attending the Nazarean Church. Life just seemed empty without a job, and there was nothing to do but listen to silly radio talk shows in the evenings.

Margaretha's thoughts turned to Aunt Eva Maier, a believer in Christ. Aunt Eva, Mame's older sister, had also immigrated to Germany. She lived in Nendingen, Wurttenberg. Feeling a closer connection with her, Margaretha began corresponding with her and poured out her feelings in letters. It was eventually decided that Margaretha and Jakob would move in with Aunt Eva. Uncle Jakob gave them his blessings.

In Nendigen, Margaretha and Jakob both secured a position in the Zwingenberger Knitting Factory. It was a three-kilometer bike ride to and from the factory. Margaretha worked at a machine that knitted socks. When the two of them earned enough money to afford a monthly rent, they moved into a two-room apartment above a restaurant by the Danube River in Mülheim.

* * * * * * * * * * * * * * * * * *

EDITOR NOTE: Margaretha stated that their Yugoslavian ID passbooks were not actual passports, but a form of identification that declared them free to travel within Yugoslavia. All Yugoslavian citizens were expected to have identification on them while traveling. Margaretha also stated that if they were caught without their ID passbooks on them, they would immediately be sent to a forced labor camp.

Photo of Margaretha, Jakob, and Florina taken during the summer of 1952. Margaretha had sewed matching dresses for herself and Florina.

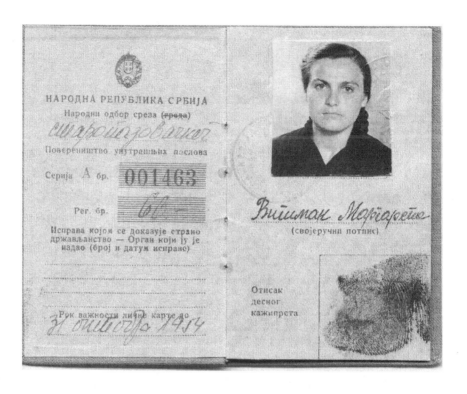

Photo of Margaretha's Yugoslavian ID passbook

28

Spiritual Freedom
1953

Easter of 1953 was extra special. Great Uncle Michael Deschner had worked through the Red Cross to sponsor Florina so she could be released from the Slovenian orphanage. How overjoyed Margaretha and Jakob were when Florina received her acceptance papers and then traveled to Germany to move in with them! Uncle Deschner served as Florina's guardian because Florina was still seventeen years old and considered a minor. He recommended that she go back to school for a year to re-learn German.

Margaretha was content living in Germany with her siblings. She was also grateful for the opportunity to attend church in nearby Tuttlingen with Aunt Eva. Even though Jakob and Florina did not show any interest in going to church, Margaretha looked forward to the bike rides there every Sunday. She felt a strong urgency to learn more about God and the Bible.

The small Tuttlingen congregation rented a large room in a hotel on the second and fourth Sundays for their church services. On the third Sunday of the month, Margaretha joined a group of people from Tuttlingen who traveled by bus to the village of Irauch. Church services were held at the Maier and Frick farms on a rotating basis. Margaretha felt blessed by the sermons and fellowship at the farms, and they always ended their meetings with a delicious and hearty dinner!

One Sunday, a visiting minister from Switzerland came to one of the farm services in Irauch. During his sermon, he referred to the Bible verse "For the time is come that judgment must begin at the house of God: and if it first begin at us, what shall the end be of them that obey not the gospel of God? And if the righteous scarcely be saved, where shall the ungodly and the sinner appear (1 Peter 4:17–18) KJV."

Margaretha was physically freed from the concentration camp, the orphanages, and Communist Yugoslavia, yet she still felt burdened. How could she expect God's forgiveness in her life, while she still clung to the hatred and bitterness that she felt towards those who had made her family suffer and die in the concentration camp? With God's grace Margaretha repented from her sinful nature, made confession, and surrendered her heart to God.

* * * * * * * * * * * * * * * * * * * *

On November 30, 1953, one year after immigrating to Germany, Margaretha found herself sitting in a chair in front of the Tuttlingen congregation. Members from Irauch, and even a busload of people from the Ballingen Church had come to hear Margaretha's testimony of faith. Three elders were present: Brothers Heinrich Muller, Franz Obmann, and Otto Baer.

Margaretha's testimony of her conversion experience began with her first exposures to the Bible. She shared with the members present her early years of going to church with Mame in Neu Pasua, and how she learned about Jesus dying on the cross at Calvary, and shedding His blood for the forgiveness of sins. Margaretha talked about how God worked in her life through the Holy Spirit to give her peace and a desire to be baptized.

Aunt Eva bought Margaretha a white dress to wear for her baptism. The baptism took place in the bathroom of a hotel room. Of course the whole congregation couldn't all fit into the bathroom, but they all stood in support just outside the doorway.

The baptismal service began with a hymn, and then the minister said a prayer. Everyone listened as Margaretha made a promise to stay true and faithful to God all the days of her life. Elder Otto Baer submerged her into the bathtub water, baptizing her in the name of the Father, the Son, and the Holy Ghost. A prayer of consecration followed, with the traditional laying on of hands by the elder for the Holy Spirit to be sealed forever in Margaretha's heart.

After the worship service, Margaretha was surprised and overjoyed to see Liese Jung and Else Matheis. Liese and Else were two of her Neu Pasuan schoolmates! She had not seen them since fleeing day. They, like Margaretha, had also become part of the Nazarean faith and were now living in Ballingen, Germany.

29

Voyage Across the Atlantic
1954 – 1957

J akob vacationed in Freiburg. He decided to remain in Freiburg after the owner of the hotel where he was staying offered him a job. In the meantime, Margaretha and Florina lived in the apartment in Mülheim. When they found out that Aunt Elisabeth and her children moved to Ballingen, they made a decision to move there too.

While living in Freiburg for some time, Jakob began to feel unchallenged. He had no permanent roots in Germany, and he thought about going to Canada. Boasting about its "open border policy", Canada was encouraging Europeans to immigrate there.

Some of the Wittmann relatives had already moved to Canada, including Aunt Margaretha and Uncle Johann Falkenberger and their family. They had settled in the city of Kitchener, Ontario, where the majority of the people were of German descent. Kitchener was originally called Berlin, but the name was changed around WWI because it sounded too German. Uncle Andreas and Aunt Elisabeth Betsch were within a reasonable driving distance from Kitchener. Their family had immigrated to the United States, settling in Mansfield, Ohio.

* * * * * * * * * * * * * * * * * * *

Jakob received his Canadian immigration papers in April, 1957. He boarded a ship that took him across the Atlantic Ocean to a harbor in Montreal, Quebec. From there he traveled with the train to Kitchener, Ontario. He moved in with his cousin Hilda Falkenburger-Baumann and her husband Matthias.

In Jakob's first letter to Margaretha and Florina, he described the beautiful Canadian landscape and the "land of opportunity." He wrote about how cheap a bunch of bananas were compared to their price in Germany. Jakob tried persuading them to immigrate to Canada. He promised that he'd get an apartment for the three of them, and together they'd be a happy family.

How Margaretha loved bananas—she would pinch her pennies to afford even one! But there were so many questions to consider about journeying across the ocean to this strange country. Besides, neither of them even knew a word of English or French.

After praying for God's direction, Margaretha was at peace about her decision to immigrate to Canada. She and Florina began filling out the required paperwork. They missed Jakob and longed for the three of them to be together.

* * * * * * * * * * * * * * * * * *

Margaretha and Florina didn't have to wait very long. In only three months they received their Canadian immigration paperwork. They sold their few possessions and managed to collect enough money to pay for their ship fares.

On November 1, 1957, Margaretha and Florina took the train to Bremen, Germany. In Bremen, they boarded a ship called *Seven Seas*. This small ship would take them across the Atlantic Ocean to a vast and multicultural country.

Seven Seas sailed smoothly away from the Bremen harbor, but it wasn't very long before the waves in the deeper water began to rock the boat. At first the rocking motion made Margaretha feel a little queasy. Then the queasiness developed into full-blown seasickness. It just wouldn't let up. The awful feeling lasted for hours.

The voyage across the Atlantic took eleven days. On more days than not, Margaretha was so sick that she wished she would die. At times *Seven Seas* passengers even had to be fastened down on their bunks. Tables, chairs, and anything that moved were also tied down to prevent them from toppling overboard.

On November 11, *Seven Seas* finally made it to the harbor in Quebec City, Canada. Although Quebec City wasn't their final destination, the *Seven Seas* would remain in the port for a great portion of the day. Margaretha and Florina were among the many passengers who got off the ship to stretch their legs and get a quick preview of their new homeland.

Out in the streets, the girls took in the new sights. There were so many large vehicles with such bright colors—red and yellow and green! The chatter of English and French and all of the other immigrants' languages was confusing. They were glad, however, to get a break from the ship before reboarding.

Seven Seas continued up the St. Lawrence Seaway to a harbor by Montreal, Quebec. In Montreal, the girls purchased train tickets that took them to Toronto, Ontario. From there, the girls made another connection to the city of Kitchener.

By the time Margaretha and Florina arrived at the Kitchener Train Station, it was already 1:00 a.m., and the sky was dark and chilly. The girls were apprehensive; they were alone in a strange country among people who spoke foreign languages. And besides their few belongings, they had only a piece of paper with Aunt Margaretha Falkenberger's address on it.

Margaretha handed the piece of paper to a taxi cab driver. He motioned for the two of them to climb into the back seat. While they were driving, the girls glanced out the windows at the houses and other cars that they passed by. "I sure hope she comes to the door when we get there," Florina said anxiously. The girls had made arrangements to spend the night at Aunt Margaretha's and Uncle Johann's house.

"We'll keep knocking until she does," Margaretha replied. "We don't have any other choice. Florina, do you have any money left?"

"Just these few coins," Florina said as she handed them to her sister.

Margaretha opened her coin purse and began counting. "These are all I've got left. What do you think the taxi driver is going to charge us?" The young women fretted between themselves. There was nothing they could do—even their belongings didn't have much value.

How surprised and relieved Margaretha and Florina were when the taxi driver interrupted their conversation. "Whatever amount of money you came up with is just fine with me," he said in German. The taxi driver had empathized with their plight, and he told the girls that he was happy to help them out. How thankful Margaretha was for God's provision.

The taxi pulled off to the curb in front of their relatives' house. Margaretha and Florina thanked the cab driver and handed him all of their coins. They gathered their small pieces of luggage and made their way to the house. After knocking several times, Cousin Liese opened the door to greet them.

Margaretha glanced back to the street; the taxi was just starting to pull away from the curb. It seemed that the kind driver had patiently waited to make sure that the girls had found the right place. Margaretha said a silent prayer of thanks to the Lord for His guidance and protection.

Margaretha, Jakob, and Florina
Photo taken in the spring of 1957, just prior to Jakob's
immigration to Canada.

247

Florina and Margaretha on the Seven Seas ship
November, 1957.

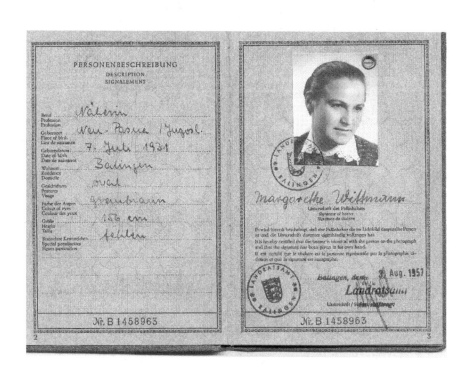

German Passport

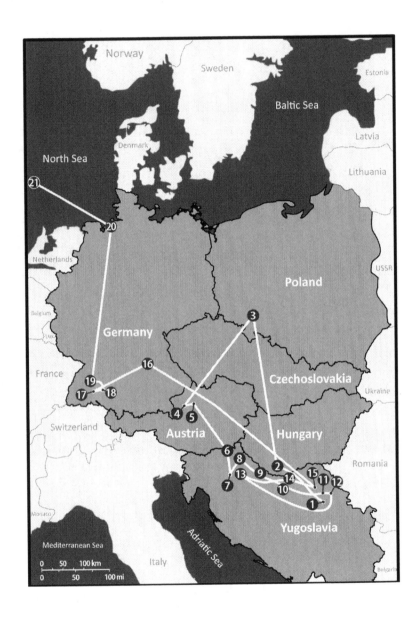

Margaretha's Journey
from Birthplace to Arrival in Canada

1. Neu Pasua, Yugoslavia
2. Pećs, Hungary
3. Region of Schlesien, Germany
4. St. George, Austria
5. Reid, Austria
6. Maribor, Yugoslavia
7. Zagreb, Yugoslavia
8. Varaždin, Yugoslavia
9. Velika Pisanica, Yugoslavia
10. Krndia, Yugoslavia
11. Sremska Mitovica, Yugoslavia
12. Debeljaca, Yugoslavia
13. Zagreb, Yugoslavia
14. Osijek, Yugoslavia
15. Beška, Yogoslavia
16. Landersdorf (Province of Bayern), Germany
17. Nendingen, Germany
18. Műhlheim, Germany
19. Balingen, Germany
20. Bremerhafen, Germany
21. Quebec City, Canada

Epilogue

Epilogue

Vladimir and Margaretha first met each other in 1958 at Niagara Falls, Ontario. Both of them had traveled to the Falls with their Nazarean Church youth groups. Vladimir lived in an apartment in Toronto; he moved there after being laid off from his Chrysler Corporation job in Windsor. Margaretha shared an apartment in Kitchener with her brother Jakob and sister Florina. As Vladimir and Margaretha talked with each other during their outing, they realized that they had more in common than their faith in God. They were born in the same country, and they had also crossed through the same city of Sremska, Mitrovica, Yugoslavia during their WWII experiences.

After several more encounters at church functions, Vladimir found himself attracted to Margaretha. He felt a desire to marry her, but he wanted to make sure that he was directed by God. After receiving affirmation, Vladimir followed the Nazarean Church's tradition of relaying his proposal through the church elder. But since the Kitchener church lacked an elder, Adam Winterstein, a minister, shared the proposal with Margaretha. She also turned to the Lord in prayer before giving her response. Margaretha was assured that it was God's will for her to marry Vladimir after reading the Bible verse "Delight thyself also in the Lord; and he shall given thee the desires of thine heart. Commit thy way unto the Lord; trust also in him; and he shall bring it to pass (Psalm 37:4-5) KJV."

Vladimir gave Margaretha money to purchase some fabric for a wedding dress, and Gena Jokic sewed the dress for her. They were married on February 22, 1959 at the Apostolic Christian Nazarean Church in Kitchener. Rada Gicanov and Margaretha's cousin Liese Falkenburger stood as witnesses, along with their family and friends. Only one week later,

Vladimir turned twenty-eight years old, and Margaretha was just a few months from her twenty-eighth birthday. The couple began their married life with the wedding gifts and very little else between them. They lived in a furnished apartment in Toronto for a short time before moving to Kitchener.

Vladimir and Margaretha have resided in the Kitchener-Waterloo region ever since, and are currently living in St. Jacobs, Ontario. God has blessed them with 12 children: Astrid (Henry Schlauch), Aron (Tamara McCarty), Carola (Jay Schlatter), Lydia (Todd Graf), Wanda (Roscoe Hilty), Ingrid, Rosanne (Daniel Graf), Magdalena (Clint Schmidt), W. David, Johanna, Barbara (Arlyn Zollinger), and Miriam (Nathan Reutter). Every time Margaretha realized she was expecting another child, she gave thanks for the miracle of surviving the Mitrovica concentration camp and still being able to lead a normal, healthy life.

Seven of Vladimir and Margaretha's daughters live in the United States. The rest of their children live near them in Ontario. There are more than 30 grandchildren and great-grandchildren. Their names can be viewed in the Fortenbacher Genealogy.

* * * * * * * * * * * * * * * * * * *

Jakob Wittman, Margaretha's brother, married Karin Gaudian in May of 1960. Karin passed away on December 24, 2010. There are three children from their marriage: Irene (Mark Bannon), Jacob, and Nicole. Jakob enjoys spending time with his four grandchildren Jamie Lee, Kyle, Melissa, and Nathan. He lives in Waterloo, only a few kilometers from his two sisters.

Florina married Otto Neu in July, 1959. She and Otto had one son named Edwin who tragically drowned at the young age of sixteen. Otto passed away in 2005. Florina lives in Kitchener, and the three siblings see each other frequently.

* * * * * * * * * * * * * * * * * * * *

The Fortenbacher family eventually all immigrated to Canada. They initially lived in Windsor, Ontario, but better job opportunities brought them to other cities.

Dragutin currently lives in Kitchener with his common-law wife Veronica. He has three daughters from a previous marriage: Edith (Steve Paul), Linda (Steve Kovacs), and Helga (Gerry Rife). He also has two granddaughters, Falon and Nicole.

Ana Ivkovic lives in the city of Toronto. Her husband Zivojin passed away in September, 2013. Their three children all reside in the Toronto area: a daughter, Radmila, and two sons, Dusko (Silvia Wannan) and Zoran (Heidi Reznik). Anna has one granddaughter named Sasha.

Rozalia moved to Hamilton, Ontario where she met and married Jozsef Varga. They live in the nearby city of Stoney Creek. They have three sons: Jozsef, Tibor, and Steven (Shannon Pyles). Rozalia and Jozsef have two grandsons named Levente and Attila, and one granddaughter named Sofia Rose.

Maritza lives in Kitchener. She remained single, and took care of her parents until they passed away. Franjo Fortenbacher passed away April 6, 1988 at the age of eighty-four, and Katarina passed away on May 12, 1997 at the age of eighty-seven.

Wedding photo of Vladimir and Margaretha Fortenbacher
taken on February 22, 1959

Photo of combined Wittmann and Fortenbacher families
L - R: Ana and Zivojin Ivkovic, Florina Wittmann,
Dragutin Fortenbacher,
Margaretha and Vladimir Fortenbacher (in center),
Joe and Rozalia Varga,
Jakob Wittmann, Maritza Fortenbacher
Katarina and Franjo Fortenbacher are seated in the front row

Fortenbacher Genealogy

Vladimir and Margaretha Fortenbacher
m. February 22, 1959

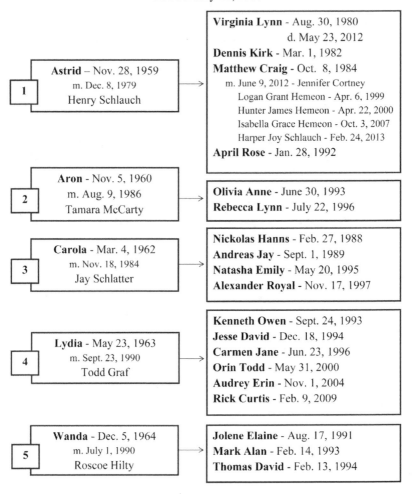

1

Astrid – Nov. 28, 1959
m. Dec. 8, 1979
Henry Schlauch

→

Virginia Lynn - Aug. 30, 1980
              d. May 23, 2012
Dennis Kirk - Mar. 1, 1982
Matthew Craig - Oct. 8, 1984
  m. June 9, 2012 - Jennifer Cortney
    Logan Grant Hemeon - Apr. 6, 1999
    Hunter James Hemeon - Apr. 22, 2000
    Isabella Grace Hemeon - Oct. 3, 2007
    Harper Joy Schlauch - Feb. 24, 2013
April Rose - Jan. 28, 1992

2

Aron - Nov. 5, 1960
m. Aug. 9, 1986
Tamara McCarty

→

Olivia Anne - June 30, 1993
Rebecca Lynn - July 22, 1996

3

Carola - Mar. 4, 1962
m. Nov. 18, 1984
Jay Schlatter

→

Nickolas Hanns - Feb. 27, 1988
Andreas Jay - Sept. 1, 1989
Natasha Emily - May 20, 1995
Alexander Royal - Nov. 17, 1997

4

Lydia - May 23, 1963
m. Sept. 23, 1990
Todd Graf

→

Kenneth Owen - Sept. 24, 1993
Jesse David - Dec. 18, 1994
Carmen Jane - Jun. 23, 1996
Orin Todd - May 31, 2000
Audrey Erin - Nov. 1, 2004
Rick Curtis - Feb. 9, 2009

5

Wanda - Dec. 5, 1964
m. July 1, 1990
Roscoe Hilty

→

Jolene Elaine - Aug. 17, 1991
Mark Alan - Feb. 14, 1993
Thomas David - Feb. 13, 1994

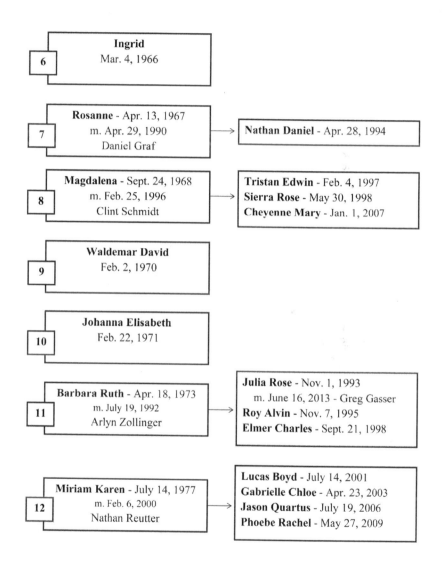

6 | **Ingrid**
Mar. 4, 1966

7 | **Rosanne** - Apr. 13, 1967
m. Apr. 29, 1990
Daniel Graf
→ **Nathan Daniel** - Apr. 28, 1994

8 | **Magdalena** - Sept. 24, 1968
m. Feb. 25, 1996
Clint Schmidt
→ **Tristan Edwin** - Feb. 4, 1997
Sierra Rose - May 30, 1998
Cheyenne Mary - Jan. 1, 2007

9 | **Waldemar David**
Feb. 2, 1970

10 | **Johanna Elisabeth**
Feb. 22, 1971

11 | **Barbara Ruth** - Apr. 18, 1973
m. July 19, 1992
Arlyn Zollinger
→ **Julia Rose** - Nov. 1, 1993
m. June 16, 2013 - Greg Gasser
Roy Alvin - Nov. 7, 1995
Elmer Charles - Sept. 21, 1998

12 | **Miriam Karen** - July 14, 1977
m. Feb. 6, 2000
Nathan Reutter
→ **Lucas Boyd** - July 14, 2001
Gabrielle Chloe - Apr. 23, 2003
Jason Quartus - July 19, 2006
Phoebe Rachel - May 27, 2009

Note from Vladimir and Margaretha's Children

When we got off the school bus at the end of the day, we'd come into the house complaining, "We're starving!" Mom often said to us, "Children, you have no idea what starving really means." All of us can attest that there was never a day where we missed a meal, and there were always clothes on our backs and a roof over our heads. We learned rather quickly not to waste any food.

It is ironic that so much of our parents' lives were spent providing food on the table for their own version of *Cheaper by the Dozen*. Pop raised chickens and rabbits for meat on our small farm in Mannheim, Ontario. He also managed our large garden and supervised the planting, watering, hoeing, and picking of produce. We have memories of shucking peas by the bushel baskets, and helping Mom can about 260 quarts of tomato juice in a season.

Pop was serious during our childhood, and "steadfast" would be the best word to describe him. No wonder he was strict; what a nightmare to think about raising 12 children! He tried his best to be the spiritual leader of our home. At the dinner table he would read a chapter from the Bible, and at bedtime he would gather us all together to recite the Lord's Prayer and sing hymns. On hot summer days Pop took us to Schneider's Park Beach—$1.00 a carload in those days—but only after we finished our garden jobs and other miscellaneous chores.

Mom was more cheerful, and she could laugh until the tip of her nose turned white. If there was one word to describe her, it would be "resilient." Mom never complained; she just went about her work of tending to her husband and 12 children. As teenagers, we recall commenting to each other on how Mom seemed to have more energy than any of her daughters. Mom's jobs were endless—from cooking the meals and baking, to doing neverending laundry piles. We had no idea until later in life that many times Mom had gotten up in the middle of the night to catch up on sewing our new matching dresses!

Pop and Mom were not materialistic and they gave us words of wisdom that helped shape our lives. They personally lived out the Bible passage "Lay not up for yourselves treasures upon earth, where moth and rust doth corrupt, and where thieves break through and steal: But lay up for yourselves treasures in heaven, where neither moth nor rust doth corrupt, and where thieves do not break through nor steal: For where your treasure is, there will your heart be also (Matthew 6:19–21) KJV." Even though they had so much taken away from them, they continued to give. Pop and Mom were the king and queen of hospitality and have hosted hundreds of people in their home.

If life gives you stinging nettle, make tea! As Vladimir and Margaretha's lives testify, they didn't let the pain of WWII cause bitterness or resentment. Forgiveness was the key factor that helped them heal and move on in their lives. They can also attest that true freedom from sin and unforgiveness is found only in surrendering the heart and mind to God and His son Jesus Christ.

"Ask, and it shall be given you; seek, and ye shall find; knock and it shall be opened unto you."

(Matthew 7:7) KJV

264

Photo taken in 1969 with eight Fortenbacher children
L – R: Astrid, Aron (holding Magdalena), Carola, Lydia,
Wanda, Ingrid, and Rosanne

Photo taken in 1970 with nine Fortenbacher children
L – R: Astrid (holding W. David), Aron, Carola, Lydia, Wanda,
Ingrid, Rosanne, and Magdalena

Photo taken in 1971 with ten Fortenbacher children. Photo was
taken during Aunt Eva's visit to Canada. L – R: Astrid
(holding Johanna), Aron, Carola, Lydia, Wanda, Ingrid,
Rosanne, Magdalena, and W. David

Most recent photo of all 12 Fortenbacher children
taken June 15, 2013
L - R: Astrid, Aron, Carola, Lydia, Wanda, Ingrid, Rosanne,
Magdalena, W. David, Johanna, Barbara, and Miriam

Note from Kendra

When I approached the Fortenbachers about the possibility of recording their experiences in a book, I did not perceive how involved and lengthy the project would become; nor did I fathom how much their willingness to share would personally affect my life. Exposing yourself by putting your life's experiences into a book is not something that everyone would do. Sharing difficult experiences from the past is not easy, and many choose to not submit themselves to remembering the pain from the past. However, Vladimir and Margaretha have been willing to share so that we can learn, and I am indebted to them for their openness. After reading their story, if you compare it to your life and allow the lessons to sink in, perhaps you will feel the same.

When my day as a farm wife has been long, and the children are getting cranky, and getting all eight of them settled into bed becomes complicated, I picture that Kinder Kamp in Mitrovica, and I'm so thankful to be tucking them in with pillows and sheets and mattresses instead of wood boards and a bit of straw.

When someone has been unkind to me, and I'm tempted to retaliate, I remind myself of the examples in *Stinging Nettle* of how ill will becomes addicting, but forgiveness fosters peace. The young corporal in charge of the concentration camp wanted to "get back" at the Germans; yet all his hatred and cruelty only put him into a further frenzy that could not satisfy his hunger for revenge. In contrast, Margaretha could have justified ill will towards those who mistreated the Germans, but instead she chose forgiveness through a spiritual rebirth and was satisfied with a lasting peace.

When I wonder how the message of salvation can spread and how those in war-torn lands will find the way of peace, then I think of how Vladimir's dad met a believer and learned of the Word of God. And I realize again how salvation's plan is extended through love, and how God can make Himself known to any who humbly seek Him.

When our children study the Holocaust in their history books, I am driven to explain to them the rest of the story, which so few students know about. The truth is that while the Jews in Germany were being liberated at the end of WWII, the people of German descent living in Yugoslavia, Romania, and Hungary were being rounded up and put in concentration camps to be obliterated.

And finally, when I have a project that simply refuses to come to completion, even though I prioritize it as a "good thing" that "needs done," I think of *Stinging Nettle*. I remember how strongly I felt that it should be completed, yet also felt the limit of my time and insight . . . it needed someone closer to their family to accurately finish the details and make the final decisions on writing style, what names to use, etc. After exhausting my resources, I placed it before God in prayer, and then, in His hands and in His timing, the book was brought to completion under the direction of Carola Schlatter, a daughter of Vladimir and Margaretha Fortenbacher.

In Memory of Relatives Who Lost Their Lives in Concentration Camps

Margaretha Alter-Wittmann (July, 1945)
Elisabeth Wittmann (December 19, 1945)
Jakob Wittmann (December 21, 1945)
Elisabeth Wittmann (end of December, 1945)
Florina Wittmann (January 6, 1946)
Friedrich Wittmann (January 21, 1946)
Johann Wittmann (January 26, 1946)
Jakob Wittmann (February 3, 1946)
Friedrich (Fritz) Wittmann (February 27, 1946)
Magdalena Deschner-Wittmann (March 3, 1946)
Herta Wittmann (March 13, 1946)
Magdalena Wittmann (November 1946)

And God shall wipe away all tears from their eyes;
and there shall be no more death, neither sorrow,
nor crying, neither shall there be any more pain:
for the former things are passed away.
Behold, I make all things new.
He that overcometh shall inherit all things;
and I will be his God, and he shall be my son.

Revelation 21:4–7

Concentration Camp Survivors

Margaretha Wittmann (Hans Gal)
Margaretha (Gretle) Wittmann (Vladimir Fortenbacher)
Jakob Wittmann (Karin Gaudian)
Florina Wittmann (Otto Neu)
Elisabeth (Liese) Wittmann (John Mohan)
Katharina Wittmann (Emilio Nunziato)
Johann Wittmann
Barbara Wittmann (Reiner Wieland)
Elisabeth Wittmann (Andreas Betsch)
Jakob Betsch
Florina Betsch (Michael Baumann)
Reinholdt Betsch (Mary Elisabeth)

References

Apostolic Christian Church (Nazarean). "Church History."
    Accessed 6 March 2012.
    http://acc-nazarean.org/Church%20History/church-
    history-5.html.

Apostolic Christian Church of America. "Origin of the Church."
    Accessed 6 March 2012.
    http://apostolicchristian.org/about_origin.php.

Hudjetz-Loeber, Dr. Irmgard. *Neu Pasua Heimatbuch*.
    Reutlingen: Reinhardt & Reicheneker, Grafischer
    Betrieb, 7434 Riederich, 1989.

"Map of the Danube River." Accessed 21 January 2013.
    http://danube-research.com/map.

"The Resistance Movement in Yugoslavia." Accessed 28
    January 2012.
    http://www.hsitorylearningsite.co.uk/resistance-
    movement-in-yugoslavi.htm.

Ruegger, Herman. *Apostolic Christian Church History: Volume
    I*. Chicago: Apostolic Christian Publishing Co., 1949.

Schmidt, Frank. "The Demise of the Ethnic Groups of Hungary,
    Romania and Yugoslavia."   Accessed 21 May 2012.
    http://molidorf.com/theextermination.html.

4

"Stinging nettle." Retrieved 2 July 2013.
http://umm.edu/health/medical/altmed/herb/stinging-nettle.

Timelines of History. "Timeline Yugoslavia." Accessed 11 December 2012.
http://timelines.ws/countries/YUGOSLAVIA.HTML.